His Mother!

Women Write about Their Mothers-in-law

with Humor, Frustration, and Love

Laura P.
Valtorta (p. 109)
I grew up in
Watertown, NY

Compiled & Edited by

Sandy F. Richardson

Southern Sass Publishing Alliances

Published by Southern Sass Publishing Alliances
Sumter, SC
www.SouthernSassPublishingAlliances.com

ISBN: 0692757929
ISBN-13:978-0692757925

DEDICATION

To all the mothers who courageously take on the role of *his* mother!

Acknowledgements

Some fifteen years ago, Dinah Johnson and I shared lunch and a gooey chocolate dessert in a small café next to a railroad track in Columbia, South Carolina. We talked of family, friendship, and books, and shared horror stories and heartaches about our mothers-in-law.

"We should write a book," she said.

"Yeah, we should," I replied.

So the seed grew, as did other responsibilities, and eventually I found myself sole custodian of our baby book. She insists she wants no credit, but I know that without her, I would have never dared. So thank you my forever friend for your idea, your courage, and your support. I love you.

I also send much love and heart-felt thanks to:

- The contributors to this book: For their courage in sharing their stories and for their patience over these years as we prepared for publication.

- Peg Bell, Dave Thompson, Michelle Ross, Kathy China, Sherry Fasano, Dale Barwick, Susan Osteen, and Cathie Pelletier: For their individual friendship and encouragement and for the sharing of their own writing as well as individual readings, comments, and suggestions for this book.

- Phil, Christy, Jay, and Callison: For their forbearance with my spacey-ness, preoccupations, and weekends in lockdown.

- Smokey, Charlie, and my sweet, sweet Riley, who now supervises from heaven: For warm, encouraging purrs, head-butts, long hours of supervision from the top of the printer, and especially for their insistence that treats and naps are necessary parts of the process.

Without each of you, I could not do this thing I so love to do.

~Sandy

CONTENTS

CONTENTS

INTRODUCTION

At some point in life, most of us have sung along with the lyrics of Ernie K-Doe's popular 60s song "Mother-in-Law." Ernie is quoted as having said the song would last until "the end of Earth because someone is always getting married." [1] For a good many of us, the foreboding words of his song hover warningly, especially when we begin to consider the pros and cons of having a mother-in-law of our own.

In addition, books, movies, television shows, quotes, anecdotes, historical notations, poems, and even plant names world-wide support the long history of the difficulties between mothers-in-law and their children's spouses.

For instance, do you know about a Spanish plant known as *silla de la suegra*? This plant produces a stunning flower only one day a year. It belongs to the cactus family. "Beautiful," they say. But translated, the plant's name means "mother-in-law chair."

Another plant, the *Monstera deliciosa* of the *sansevieria* family, produces showy, deep green leaves and is quite unique in appearance. However, care in handling is prescribed. The plant contains a poison that causes much discomfort by swelling the tongue and creating an intense, burning irritation inside and outside the mouth, not to mention that it can hinder swallowing and induce severe drooling and vomiting. Some people know it as "Snake Plant," but others call it "Mother-in-law Tongue."

As for historic cultural views worldwide, opinions on the mother-in-law appear to substantiate the need for wariness inherent in this age-old role (except, of course, Ruth's beautiful words to Naomi in chapter one of the Book of Ruth in the *Holy Bible*). For example, in Russia many young married couples live with the parents of one or the other due to a shortage of available rental properties, and for years, jokes and bizarre anecdotes about in-law relationships have been extremely popular there.[2]

China, as well, holds to the pattern. The mother-in-law reigns as an integral part of the customs and lore. The Chinese mother usually plays a dominant and decisive role in the family, and the relationship is one of submission by the daughter to the mother or mother-in-law. Most sons and daughters feel a duty to continue this relationship after marriage. In more recent years, programs such as the "Mother-in-Law Strategy" have been developed in such places as Shenzhen, Chengdu, Ningbo, and Shanghai to attract mothers to the city, thus bringing the young, educated sons and daughters with them to help fill the human resource needs of the economic and technologic boom in these cities.[3]

Pakistani mothers-in-law often have strong control over women's lives and can even influence the number of children in the marriage.[4] And in Korea, couples live with and serve the husband's parents after marriage with the mother in-law granting the young wife a brief return to her own family shortly before giving birth and allowing a month's stay afterwards.[5]

Western and European wives fare better in that they are seldom forced or expected to live with their in-laws, but the influence of the mother-in-law remains a powerful factor affecting many aspects of family life.

In her performances as a member of the educational theatre company known as *Heroic Women You Can Talk To*, Kate Carney portrays Rachel Walker, Paul Revere's mother-in-law. Set in 1789, the portrayal presents Revere's mother-in-law preparing for a visit from President George Washington who is to come to the tavern and inn she owns. Walker and several lady friends had previously organized a riot over coffee prices, and during her preparations for Washington's visit, Walker presents a diatribe on those issues, as well as on the Boston Massacre, the tea destruction, and Paul's famous midnight ride. True to mother-in-law lore, Walker complains that her daughter must raise and care for Paul's six older children in addition to the eight they produced together. Revere's dear mother-in-law frowns on the unfairness of the situation and makes her stance clearly known: Revere's riding too often keeps him away from home and his responsibilities.[6]

However, a small shift in attitude began to appear in the late 1930s. "The Tactless Texan" (aka Globe-News Publisher Gene Howe) carelessly made an unfortunate public remark concerning his mother-in-law. In an attempt to repair the damage, he apologized and declared March 5 as Mother-in-Law day to honor these special women. Amarillo's society matrons whole-heartedly supported the move which resulted in a huge parade including such dignitaries as First Lady Eleanor Roosevelt as guest of honor. Finally in 1981 (the wheels of justice *do* turn slowly), the US Congress officially made the fourth Sunday in October the official, national Mothers-in-Law Day to be celebrated each year.

But even as late as 2003, conflict about the relationship endured. India's Prime Minister tactfully reminded daughters-in-law to remember they themselves might become mothers-in-law in the future. And in her wonderful bold and frank way, author Camille Russo smilingly warned mothers-in-law to take heed: "Your daughter-in-law may have the final say on which nursing home you'll be sent to!"

The narratives, stories, poems, and essays contributed to *His Mother!* overwhelmingly support and document the widespread and varying perceptions of the mother-in-law/daughter-in-law relationship. The writers represent a range of age groups, religious backgrounds, ethnic and national cultures, and economic and educational experiences. And while a few accounts depict the darker side of the relationship, most of the writings speak of strong bonds with this often-maligned presence, the mother-in-law. Contrary to common lore, most exhibit a sense of friendship, loyalty, love, and hope.

So whatever the state of your relationship with your mother-in-law, I hope the readings in *His Mother!* offer encouragement to those who need it and hope to those who prepare for this complex and sacred union. (And remember: a little humor never hurts.)

~Sandy Richardson

Mrs. Kalesperis
by Kirsten Guenther

Mrs. Kalesperis: Orange County socialite, tall, thin, highlighted blonde who doesn't eat. Mother of two boys, two girls, plus two Rottweilers named Bill and Agnes which she dresses up in coordinating bandanas for dinner parties. Enjoys baking pumpkin muffins and sucking the salt off of pistachio shells...though she does not eat the actual nut. She's addicted to Disney paraphernalia, and she is extremely involved in everybody else's business. At the age of twenty-eight, married once before to a man with whom she had a baby girl, she married for the second time, a very Greek man. She is my mother-in-law.

*****

Trying to avoid breaking my neck on the taut seat belt, I reach into the back seat for the half-eaten bag of dried apricots. I am starving. My boyfriend Brian and I begin our three-hour drive from our college campus in Los Angeles to San Diego for a surprise romantic weekend he planned.

"And part of the surprise is you get to meet Mom and Dad finally. We'll stop in Laguna for dinner on the way," he added.

Twenty minutes into the drive, I have already consumed an entire bag of dried bananas, half a bag of apricots, and three quarters of a jar of peanut butter. I'm feeling a little nauseated, though I continue to gorge myself, despite the fact that I have a slight allergy to peanuts. I usually prefer almond butter, but the corner market where we stopped had none on the shelves, and offered only corn nuts or peanut butter.

Brian rests his right hand on my left knee and offers me a reassuring smile, which does not make me feel any better, but it is a loving gesture. It irritates me when Brian takes his hands off the wheel when he drives because he has a little attention span problem. He is not the type who can handle more than one activity at once. I put my hand on his, bring it up to my lips, and kiss his right index finger. I then strategically place it back on the wheel and reach into the back seat for the black licorice.

Brian tells me about the church group (Greek Orthodox) that his mother heads and that she's always entertaining kids at their home. His mother actually had an entire wing of the house redecorated in various Disney themes for the children and brought in a big-screen TV so they could watch Disney movies without straining their eyes.

Apparently, the Kalesperis family is really into the Disney thing. In fact, Brian's older sister Andrea is auditioning for the touring company of *Beauty and the Beast* the next Tuesday, for the sixth time. This is somewhat comforting, since I'm relatively up to date on the Disney films, although I missed *Aladdin II*. The classic *Sleeping Beauty* remains my all-time favorite with the ever-so-dreamy Prince and the way he fights off the dragon and then tears down the great mass of thorns. He surely has the strength of Beowulf.

I've been to Disneyland about fifty times with my grandparents who live in Pasadena. My Grandpa Roland entertains himself on the Pirates of the Caribbean by making obscure bird calls he learned in the army. He makes me laugh. My Grandma Roland, embarrassed, whacks his knee the entire ride and refuses him a Kleenex when he requests one, all while she fights a smile.

Okay. Disney, I can do. At least Mrs. Kalesperis and I will have something to talk about at dinner.

Forty-five minutes later, we enter Laguna, a residential area where huge homes tower over small lots with palm trees planted in every yard. At 5PM, the sun begins to lower in the sky reflecting off of the intense gardens of white, pink, yellow, and orange roses. At the end of the street called "Dwarf Lane," we pull into a circular driveway surrounding the perimeter of a huge English Tudor.

Brian parks the car in front. I wait, expecting a valet, but Brian gets out of the car and removes a few bags and his laundry basket from the back seat. I don't move. I can't move. My stomach is feeling very unsettled. I really should not have eaten that peanut butter. Finally, Brian comes over to the passenger side, opens the door, and pulls me out. Again, he tries to reassure me with a smile.

My legs are reluctant to move as he continues to push me up to the door where two lemon trees are growing in Mickey and Minnie Mouse planters.

Oh God, I don't feel well. Everything I look at is wearing spots.

Brian rings the doorbell, and I hear a high-pitched squeal from inside the house. I cannot determine whether the squeals come from his overly excited mother, or if perhaps someone stepped on the tail of one of the dogs causing it to cry out in pain. Maybe Mrs. Kalesperis took one look at me through the gold drapes and is now howling at the powers that be.

The massive wood door opens revealing a tall, skinny woman in her late fifties. She wears a Ralph Lauren pink and white pinstriped button-down shirt tucked into a pair of fitted white slacks and a white belt with a gold buckle. Her strangely fat feet are forced into her white high heels. She has a massive pouf of dyed blond hair, obviously highlighted this morning. A cloud of gray eye shadow looms above her deep-set, blue eyes. Her shimmer-pink lipstick emphasizes a forced smile.

Mrs. Kalesperis grabs me immediately and pulls me into the house, hugging me while shouting, "Honey, she's here. She's here, and she's just adorable."

Her perfume or perfumes are unbearable. She smells like she walked through the scent section at Saks and sprayed every display bottle on her body. My stomach starts making loud noises, and both Mrs. Kalesperis and Brian look concerned. Two giant Rottweilers wearing matching pink scarves with yellow flowers troop into the entrance hall followed by a stout man of about sixty with a friendly bulldog's face and wearing an expensive gold watch. It's Brian's dad, Mr. Kalesperis.

Mr. Kalesperis's offensive designer cologne mixes with Mrs. Kalesperis's department store spree. The room spins. I vomit on Mr. Kalesperis' newly polished tasseled loafers.

I want to go home.

Mrs. Kalesperis rushes to the kitchen to get the paper towels while Mr. Kalesperis tries to laugh it off. I glance at myself in the mirror above the marble table with the pink flower arrangement. I am green.

I really want to go home.

I hate peanut butter.

Mrs. Kalesperis returns with a roll of paper towels decorated with little yellow bows. She hands me one and then has Mr. Kalesperis remove his shoes so she can clean them. Brian takes me into the living room to lie down before dinner.

I am surrounded by crystal and porcelain. I close my eyes to block out the light. One hour later, having rested and gotten the peanut butter out of my system, I am feeling much better. I wash up in the small half-bathroom in the entrance hall and meet Brian and his parents in the dining room. Mr. Kalesperis holds a large carving knife and leans over what appears to be a corpse. I look at Brian, appalled. We are having lamb for dinner. I've had lamb before; in fact, my mother makes it each year for Christmas dinner. However, I've never actually seen a whole cooked lamb. This lamb has wool on it.

Mrs. Kalesperis fills our plates with cucumbers and feta cheese while her husband cuts into the corpse. They tell me I am about to experience a Greek delicacy. Dinner is served. The conversation begins quite pleasantly.

"Kirsten, what is your major?

"Acting."

"Oh, that's wonderful. We'll have to come see one of your plays"... blah, blah, blah.

Everything is going well. I am charming and polite, the perfect girlfriend for their son and then....

"What faith are you? Do you go to church? No, well, would you be willing to convert?

Really, your mother is Buddhist? Does that mean you're a Democrat?"

Needless to say, I am no longer the preferred girlfriend for the son of these Greek Orthodox, Orange County Republicans.

I change the subject and ask if I will get the chance to meet Andrea. Brian's other siblings are back east, but since Andrea still lives at home at the age of twenty-six, I thought she would be at dinner. But apparently she is staying late at the dance studio tonight, rehearsing for her audition for *Beauty and the Beast* on Tuesday morning.

"Oh, really? I love *Beauty and the Beast*. I know all of the songs by heart! That's so wonderful that she's so dedica—"

Mrs. Kalesperis interrupts me from behind the lamb corpse. "Can you name the seven dwarves?"

"What?"

"Can you name all seven dwarves?"

Ahhh.... That explains the street name. I wonder if Mrs. Kalesperis chose a house on a street named "Dwarf" purely because of her Disney obsession or if she managed to have the street renamed.

"Well, hmm, let me think, I don't know, Ah... Dopey."

"That's one...."

"Uhhhh, Snoopy?"

"That's a dog," She says this with a dead-pan face.

"Okay, I usually do know them," I say and laugh a little. "I guess I'm a little rusty under pressure, you know?"

"Well, aren't we all." She looks at her husband.

What does that mean? I wonder if she's implying in front of guests that her husband can't get it up. Brian, embarrassed, clears his throat and begins to clear the table providing my escape. I jump up to help him.

I carefully collect the gold-rimmed china plates and follow Brian into the kitchen. I set them on the perfectly clean, white-tile counter and empty my napkin filled with chewed lamb corpse into the trash can. I grab Brian by the collar and threaten his life unless we leave for San Diego NOW.

Brian goes into the dining room and makes apologies that we will be unable to stay for dessert. I thank Mr. and Mrs. Kalesperis for a lovely dinner and head for the door. Mrs. Kalesperis runs after me and grabs me from behind. At first, I fear she is trying to suffocate me, but it turns out she just gives really strong hugs.

"Take care of our Brian. You're such a darling, and we'll be in touch soon."

She hates me. I climb in the car, deflated of all energy and depressed that the man I intend on marrying has Greek Orthodox parents who hate me because my mom is Buddhist (and, therefore, a Democrat) and because I thought Snoopy was a dwarf. From the car, I watch Brian kiss both of his parents good-bye. His mother whispers something in his ear while glancing at me. I hear Brian say, "I'll ask her."

He opens the car door, leans in, and gives me a kiss. "They LOVED you!"

"Oh, bullshit, Brian! That whole thing was a complete catastrophe. I threw up all over your dad's loafers, and I failed the dwarf test. Just stop it."

"No, my mom really liked you. In fact, she wants you to come back on Tuesday."

"I can't. I have rehearsal. Why does she want me to come back? So that I can throw up all over her perfect white sofa? No, wait, she wants to quiz me on the names of the fairies in *Sleeping Beauty*! I wish she had. Those I know!"

"Not exactly." Brian purses his lips, something he tends to do when he's keeping something from me or not telling the whole story. So why does Mrs. Kalesperis want me to come back.

"Why, Brian? Why does she want me to come back?!"

Apparently, every year Mrs. Kalesperis puts together an afternoon garden tea with an *Alice in Wonderland* theme for all of the children in the neighborhood. Brian plays the Mad Hatter, and Andrea usually plays Alice. However, since Andrea has her audition for *Beauty and the Beast* on Tuesday, she will be unable to attend tea. Mrs. Kalesperis has decided that I am the perfect Alice: blue-eyed and blonde.

I refuse the invitation flat out. I tell Brian that he can just tell his mother that of course I would love to do it, but I have a very important rehearsal, which is true. Our conversation ends. We go on to have a relaxing weekend that allows me to forget almost completely about dinner with Brian's parents. We do not stop in Laguna on the drive back to Los Angeles.

Monday afternoon, I am back in the swing of things in my apartment located in downtown LA. A hole the size of my head decorates the kitchen floor, and the Tamale lady comes by every morning at seven. "Tamales...tamales," my alarm sounds.

I grab a bowl of granola and then my cell phone rings. A 714 area code shows on the screen. I don't recognize the number, but still, I tell myself, it could be important. And I am expecting a call from my agent.

"Hello?"

I should know better than to answer an unidentified number. This is why I have caller ID. I should think my action through more carefully, explore all of the potential caller options, but my senses are somewhat numb because of the hunger pains in my stomach.

The voice on the other line is high-pitched and over-excited. Mrs. Kalesperis. She's calling because she wants me to come to the tea on Tuesday, dress up as Alice in Wonderland, and entertain thirty-seven children, ages four to nine.

I don't think so. I have rehearsal.

Mrs. Kalesperis does not appear to be the least surprised. It turns out that Brian has already told her about my VERY important rehearsal, but she took it upon herself to call up my director and tell him about our "family emergency" requiring my presence in Orange County on Tuesday afternoon.

I am shocked. Speechless. I say nothing. I can't even think of a response. She ends the conversation for both of us and hangs up the phone.

What am I supposed to do? I can't tell my director that my boyfriend's mom, my soon to be mother-in-law, is completely crazy, and she is forcing me to wear a petticoat and prance about with small children at a pretend tea party! And while a part of me wants to make up for the vomit incident, I figure this will surely even the score.

So. Tomorrow afternoon: four o'clock tea.

I arrive at the Kalesperis home with Brian at precisely two o'clock in order to have enough time to "learn my lines" and have my "costume fitting." So while Brian is off eating a hamburger (it takes him one and a half hours to do so), I am instructed by Mrs. Kalesperis on how to speak to young children. I'm not even offered a snack.

This is because she thinks I'm fat.

"Use soft tones in the voice. Always speak in simple vocabulary. Be playful, yet careful."

The list goes on and on. I babysat for ten years, so I think I can handle having tea with a few kids. What I can't handle, though, is the blue dress, a **SIZE 2**, which Mrs. Kalesperis is now waving in my face.

No, I don't think so.

I wear a **SIZE 6**. No way that I, at 5'8", am going to squeeze into a size two. Maybe in my dreams. But Mrs. Kalesperis assures me it will be a perfect fit. After all, it fits Andrea wonderfully. I grab the dress and step into the half-bathroom where I undress, leaving my jeans and t-shirt on the white tile floor. I unzip the dress and then sift through the petticoat and slip searching for a clear passage to the neck hole.

Found! Okay, here it goes.

I pull my head through the neck hole, careful not to mess up the *Alice in Wonderland* hair-do I had teased my hair into on the car ride over.

A few seconds later, my head is through.

I hold down the skirt with my left hand as I struggle to fit my apparently fat right arm through the poufy lace sleeve. I try holding my breath and groaning, which seems to help. One more arm to go. The left is a bit more of a struggle because the material is already straining against my chest. I move slowly to avoid tearing the sacred material.

Ten minutes later the dress is on. But it's three inches too short. The hem rests an inch above my knees, and the fake buttons sewn down the front strain against my smooshed breasts. The buttons are in serious danger of popping off at any minute.

I open the bathroom door slowly, praying Mrs. Kalesperis will not be on the other side. Coast is clear. No. Wait! Here she comes running down the hall with a plate piled high with pumpkin muffins.

"Isn't the dress *divine?*" She pops a muffin in my mouth before I can respond. She is force-feeding me.

I chew. The dough is like rubber.

Two minutes later, I am still chewing the same bite. I recall that it takes fifteen years for the body to digest a stick of gum. The muffin is looking at probably thirty.

I keep the rubber muffin in my mouth until Mrs. Kalesperis becomes occupied fiddling with the bandana on one of the Rottweilers. I spit it out in my hand, lean back into the bathroom, and toss it in the trashcan.

"Where's Brian?" I ask, looking around desperately.

I can't believe he left me alone with her.

"Hold on. Be patient. It's a surprise." The grin on Mrs. Kalesperis' face spreads so wide when she says this that I remember the clowns I had nightmares about when I was little.

"Just a second!" She ducks out of the hallway into a guestroom and returns holding Brian's hand.

At first, I do not recognize him. The black hat is so tall on his small head. His ears are so big that each one is the size of my hand, fully extended, fingers and all. The giant ears are trimmed with snow-white hair pouring out over his forehead and create a mullet effect in the back due to the compression of the hat on his neck. He wears a pinstriped turquoise-green suit with a large tie decorated with diamonds that flash every color in the rainbow.

He is the Mad Hatter.

He is—unattractive.

Mrs. Kalesperis takes our hands and walks us out into the garden. Four huge picnic tables are set up with pink and white flower arrangements for the centerpieces. They are miniature versions of the arrangement she has in the entrance hall on the marble table. Elegant white lace tablecloths are set with children's china, thirty-seven petite white cups covered with yellow roses. The children sit at the tables, perfectly straight and attentive. I have never seen children sit so still. Is it possible they have been drugged?

Somewhere a clock chimes four. Time for tea.

"Attention, children," Mrs. Kalesperis announces. "Please welcome Alice and the Mad Hatter."

All the children applaud. I am touched. They are adorable. Their eyes light up watching our every move while two of Mrs. Kalesperis's housekeepers in black and white uniforms serve the children hot cocoa and charming bite-size cakes.

I walk towards the first table where a plump girl of about six with brown locks struggles to stay on the bench. I lean over her.

Her name is Sarah. I laugh as she stuffs her face with the brown cake, which is now smeared all over her face. I spot a metal folding chair nearby which I pull up at the end of the table next to Sarah. She is in the first grade, and her favorite animal is a bear.

But suddenly several of the other children seated at the table begin to shout accusations.

"Sarah's hogging Alice."

"Sarah won't let Alice talk to me."

"Alice is mean. She doesn't like me."

Soon the entire tea party is screaming for my attention. I stand up and try to make myself more available, but it is too late. I am surrounded. They pull on my hands and arms. One child jumps up my back and yanks the ends of my hair, which really hurts. I wish they would stop.

Where are Brian and Mrs. Kalesperis? I beg the children to stop, but the little torturers won't listen. My breasts strain against my dress fabric as I move my arms to push the children away. Two children swing from the material of my skirt.

Please no! Please don't let this happen to me. But there is no stopping them.

I watch in horror as the buttons pop off the front of the dress, one by one, in slow motion. When the material across my chest begins to rip, I become desperate and fling the child from my right arm. Then I pick up my skirt and shake it, causing three children to topple backward into a pile of arms and legs.

Everyone stops. The children look up at me in shock. Tears begin to well-up in all thirty-seven pairs of eyes.

"Alice tried to kill us."

Mrs. Kalesperis has never forgiven me for ruining that afternoon's tea. I have never forgiven Brian for making me fall in love with a man who has a mother addicted to Disney.

On the very quiet ride home to Los Angeles, I found out that while I was being mauled on the lawn, Brian sat in the kitchen eating the frosting off the cupcakes with his fingers.

Needless to say, I withheld sex for the rest of the week.

In My Next Life
by Susan Doherty Osteen

 My mother-in-law and I first met on a sweltering Texas day. At the time, I was just dating her youngest son, but I will admit I was smitten with my husband-to-be and sweating more over my initial encounter with his parents than from the weather. She was already a legend to me.

Her impact started with my first date with my husband Jack. It was only lunch, and we barely knew each other, but Jack told me he had mentioned our date to his mother. He swore her first comment was, "Oh, what are we going to do with another Susan in the family!"

True, Jack's older brother *is* married to a Susan. However, it startled me that a woman in South Carolina could worry about the marriage of her son to a Texas girl whom he had just met. I was intrigued.

Her premonition was early, but on target. By the end of that first lunch, I was in love. And after two hours of Jack telling me his life story, I also felt as though I knew his entire family, especially his mother Jackie.

Two months after that memorable first date, Jack's parents flew to the Texas Hill Country to visit their baby boy and to meet me, Susan #2. Our romance was now causing actual panic in the original Susan Osteen. And there I was, that hot July day, standing in the foyer of my boyfriend's apartment and shaking hands with my future in-laws.

"It's so nice of you to drive down from Fort Worth," my future father-in-law said to me.

"Of course she did," piped in Jack, who has many wonderful, admirable qualities—modesty not being one of them. "I mean, look at me. I'm just so incredibly good looking she can't stand to be away from me."

I knew he was joking, at least mostly, but his comment caught me off guard, and I froze, not quite knowing how to respond.

But Jackie came to my rescue, the first of about a million times. She calmly walked over to me, took my hand in hers, and smiled. Then, in a thick-with-honey, South Carolina accent, she spoke.

"We have always tried to instill self confidence in our boys," she said, her blue eyes cutting a knowing glance toward her youngest son. "But I am afraid we went overboard with Jack."

I couldn't help but giggle. She had his number all right, and her comment set me at ease and made me aware of one important truth: I didn't know if Jack and I would end up together, but regardless, Jackie and I were friends.

Over time, I came to realize that Jackie possesses a wonderful gift. She is able to make whomever she is speaking with feel special and important. This talent is enhanced by her full-time job, that of keeping up with friends and acquaintances. Her purse is filled with notepads overflowing with scribbles of people's names, who their parents or grandparents were, and where they come from. No matter where we travel or what we do, she is always prepared with the history of persons we will likely meet and their subsequent connection to our family. Here's a sample:

"Now we will probably run into John Smith. He is the grandson of a dear friend of my family. We always had dinner at the Smith house when we visited Charleston when I was a girl. Old Mr. Smith was a physician and went to medical school with my daddy. He had a lovely wife, named Jane, and their son was my age and went to Episcopal. Come to think of it, his grandson Henry went to Episcopal, too. Jack, you may know some of the same people since you were at prep school at the same time. Anyway, John is a surgeon like his daddy and granddaddy. He married one of my mother's, best friend's cousin's daughter and lives back in Greenville. So we are practically family...."

And on and on and on.

Jackie, the family's unofficial historian, would read the entire history complete with names of John's children, pets, and allergies. The story of John Smith and his extended family may not seem important. But, since South Carolina is really a small-town state, a day would come when we would indeed run into him, and it's nice to know the six degrees of separation.

But for Jackie, knowing the correct name of someone's child, or keeping up with a friend's ailing mother, or remembering the name of a beloved, late golden retriever are not trivial matters. Jackie stands out from the crowd because she truly cares about the people in her life, and she makes the time to let them know how much they mean to her.

She is constantly recording important facts in notebooks and, famously, on pantyhose liners. "Save the cardboard square from inside your hose for me," she politely asks. "They are the perfect size and sturdy enough, so I can write down notes while I drive."

Her logistics are unorthodox, but they work. She can find someone's number or address quicker by sorting through the bags and boxes of notebooks and hosiery packaging faster than I can search it out on my computer or phone. She rubber-bands together four years of pocket calendars.

"In my next life," she says, *"I am going to be so organized."*

And somehow, despite the rigorous schedule of keeping up with each "dear friend" and "poor soul," she still finds time to spend with her very best friends: her dogs and horses. Jackie shows up nearly every week at the SPCA with pizzas for the staff. Her own dogs are well-bred, ill-mannered, and fiercely loved. Every time we walk into her barn, she asks the rhetorical question, "Is there any smell better than horse manure?"

"In my next life," she says, *"I am going to be a veterinarian."*

A horse lover for all of her life, at 65 she still rides several times a week. In addition to her fondness for the English saddle and the smooth gait of Tennessee Walking Horses, she is enamored with life out West, especially ranch life.

Her love for everything Western is apparent in her home. While most South Carolina ladies choose the same, tired type of French country or faux plantation décor, Jackie makes her own way. I can promise she is the only Southern Belle I know who has the grand-prize painting from the Montana State Fair hanging above her living room mantle. It is a large, elaborate oil pastel of a buffalo head, and it has real character.

"In my next life," she has told me countless times, *"I am going to be a cowgirl."*

Jackie's true love, aside from cowboys and animals, is for the singers of great American songs. An airline stewardess in the 1950s, she fell in love with the old jazz singers she would see while flying in and out of New York. Jackie is instantly enamored with anyone who can tease a Gershwin tune out of a piano or croon like Rosemary Clooney.

This love has not faded, and she spends several weeks a year in the Big Apple listening to cabaret singers reinterpret the great American songbook. Over the past several years, she has acquired somewhat of an honorary place in the cabaret royalty. While many of the singers practice their talents in small nightclubs and exist in relative obscurity, some are veterans of the stage and screen, and many are actually successful recording artists.

And there, somewhere in the mix, is Jackie, a singer at heart who can't carry a tune. However, that hasn't stopped her from being featured in *Cabaret Scenes* magazine half a dozen times, nor has it kept her from being invited to some of the industry's top shows. Jackie's position in cabaret society was solidified when several of her singer friends in New York threw her a party to celebrate her 63rd birthday. There she was, the Southern princess, surrounded by over one hundred people, some of whom had flown in from Europe. They were all there to show their admiration for Jackie.

On a couple of special occasions, my husband and I have had the wonderful opportunity to accompany my in-laws to New York. The trip is always planned around a show featuring one of her many talented friends. As we sit in the Rainbow Room or the

Firebird, Jackie seems truly in her element. Caught up in the evening's magic, she will leave her food untouched and let her rum and tonic go flat. Tapping her dainty fingers gently in time with the music, she literally glows with excitement. More than once, she has leaned across the table and whispered, *"In my next life, I'm going to be a singer."*

I have come to know Jackie as a mother, a friend, and a trusted advisor. Though I may not always agree with her opinion, I respect it, and often in hindsight, I discover how wise she really is. I also consider Jackie a teacher, one whose curriculum is based on the practice of being kind to others, regardless if they are the yardman, the plumber, the governor, or Judy Garland.

I have never met anyone who knows my mother-in-law and is not fond of her, and with the way she works a room almost everyone knows Jackie. On Sundays, we gather together for a big, after-church, extended-family lunch at the Country Club. The rest of the family is finished with dessert before Jackie has made it past the salad buffet. I used to practice good manners and wait until the hostess was seated before eating, but my husband convinced me this rule does not apply when dining with Jackie. We might all starve to death waiting.

With Jackie, food always takes a back seat to visiting. This is probably how she has stayed so fit and slim despite a steady diet of crab cakes and chicken salad croissant sandwiches. Mayonnaise and butter actually have very few calories if you talk through your lunch instead of eating it.

She can neglect her own diet, especially at a cocktail party when the act of eating hors d'oeuvres involves leaving a circle of conversation, but Jackie is famous for making sure her loved ones are well fed. If someone is sick or has a death in the family, that person receives, at the very least, a delivery of chicken salad. A close friend can expect a pecan pie, as well. And if anyone is at her house or barn at any point from ten in the morning to three in the afternoon, lunch is surely served. This holds true for family, guests, or the blacksmith making new shoes for the old horses.

Not only is Jackie a beautiful person inwardly, but she is also a striking woman. She carries herself with an air of confidence that comes from being comfortable in her own skin. Yes, she has been "nipped and tucked," but for Southern women, that is good maintenance, not vanity. Confident *and* pretty, she has amazing blue eyes and a show-stopping smile. In fact, the only thing that causes her constant worry is her fine, blonde hair, and she spends a good deal of time in salons having it fixed. The rest of the time she spends fighting any breeze that threatens to undo her 'do.

Even though I never see her look less than glamorous, Jackie's hair just may be her Achilles heel. After suffering a particularly breezy outdoor event, I can find her in the ladies room, extracting a comb and brush from the many notepads of names that fill her purse. She attacks her hair, hoping to encourage volume in the fine strands through beauty parlor tricks and sheer will. At these moments, she smiles and sighs.

"In my next life," she says, *"I will have great hair."*

I have often heard that you should not take the decision to marry lightly, since ninety percent of your happiness, or lack thereof, is dependent on your choice of spouse. I would add there should also be a consideration given to prospective in-laws. I have more than one friend whose strained relationship with her mother-in-law is the source of tension, hurt, and resentment toward her husband.

Men should come with warnings: Caution! When you marry him, you are marrying his mother, too!

So, I count myself especially lucky. Not only did I find a wonderful man to share my life, but I also had the good fortune to marry into a wonderful family. And while my dear father-in-law is the head of the family, Jackie is the undeniable heart.

In a nutshell, I love Jackie. She is truly a great lady, and I am forever grateful for the chance to know her.

I hope I am wise enough to learn from her example and grow into a woman my own family loves and respects. I want to lead a full and interesting life and include loved ones in my adventures. I want to be a good friend to my future son or daughter-in-law, and I want to be too busy having fun to ever grow old.

Like her, I want to be wise enough to give advice without being pushy, and I want to support people when they make their own decisions, which will sometimes be right and sometimes be wrong.

I hope I remember to take the time to learn people's names and histories, and make them feel special when I meet them. And I want to have friends who love me and whom I love with such a passion that I will forget to eat my chicken salad croissant.

So in my next life, I want to be Jackie.

Marian

by Kathryn Etters Lovatt

Southeastern Montana's High Plateau spreads far and wide, immense as a somber ocean at world's end. When the high plains reach the horizon, they merge into that famous sky, made bluer by contrast with the terrain's brooding palette.

To my Southern eye, this first glimpse was a dizzying sight. Void of lush vines and stretches of forests or any verdant thing I could name, this domain belonged to the coulees, arroyos, and washes that long ago laid claim to pieces of the West. The ground appeared to produce mostly hard dirt and tumbleweeds; the only crops I could see were roadside sage and greasewood, creosote, and jags of cactus. Occasionally, a surprising oasis of massive trees slipped into view. Cottonwoods know water like a divining rod and cast their deep spreading roots by any reliable trickle. They subsist on snowmelt, and despite a scarcity of rain, they breed and grow in gnarly stands.

In this cracked and fissured region, what flourishes must be able to survive searing heat, perilous cold, and precious little moisture. But like winter, this frill-free terrain bears its own stark beauty. Before long, I learned to admire the fierce, if unfamiliar, landscape. In a similar way, this is how I came to appreciate my mother-in-law, whose solemn nature perfectly matched her native state.

The day before my wedding, Marian Murphy Lovatt flew South in practical black shoes, black pants, and a blouse that looked like all the others I would ever see her wear. A few dark strands still streaked her hair, turning the thick, short mass a deep shade of vintage pewter. She stood before me at attention: feet planted, shoulders squared, hands clipped at her back. A registered nurse, who served as a WAVE in the South Pacific during WWII, a military stance somehow suited her. Without a trace of a smile or a how-do-you-do, she went over me head-to-toe determining, I suppose, if I passed muster.

Already in her seventies, she looked not so much her age as ageless, like she had been salted down and seasoned by the elements. A lifetime of glacial winds and harsh weather had scored her skin until fine lines crisscrossed her face like roads on a well-used map.

Unlike my own mother, who pampered her delicate skin and resented every wrinkle, Marian never grumbled about the signs of time. She knew better than to resist what couldn't be changed and saved her energy for what could. A highline ranch that backed up to the Missouri River breaks surely helped to shape her stoic character.

At fourteen, Marian's father, Dan Murphy, sailed out of Ireland and into the dream of America. He worked his way from New York City westward, and once there, he became a genuine cowboy down to chaps and leather gauntlets. He rode the cattle trail out of Texas for the outfit with the XIT brand, letters nearly impossible for cattle rustlers to alter.

But at the turn of the twentieth century, when the government offered wild land in the Montana Territory to homesteaders, he married his sweetheart from back home, gathered his savings and set out to stake a claim. A man who understood the value of water, he chose tracts with springs and branches and disregarded the borders of broken ground and badlands. Those, he thought he could handle, and he did.

At its peak, the Murphy spread grazed 5000 head of sheep on eight sections, or roughly 5000 unconstrained acres. Once fences started going up in the mid-twenties, Murphy began to switch over to cattle and horses. No matter. There was work enough to go around for him and his wife, eight surviving offspring, plus everybody in the bunkhouse, whether cowpokes or sheepherders.

Marian, the oldest girl, learned early to ride and roundup, to shear and brand. She came to know the amount of food required to sustain men riding horses all day and mending fences, collecting sheep, or driving livestock. Daily, she helped bake yeast bread, cook beans, slabs of beef or legs of mutton, can, nurse the bum lambs, and watch her younger siblings. Midday, she carried jars of afternoon tea to the pasture. Somewhere in all of this, she completed her school lessons.

This was a land of not only hard work but also of hardship. Big brothers died of no one really knew what; premature twins set by the woodstove couldn't be saved. Until spring, a grave couldn't be dug in the frozen ground. Living on a Montana ranch meant tough work and tough truths.

Marian held her upbringing in high regard, but she wanted to go out on her own. She longed to travel; she dreamed of adventures. Her heart, she let her parents know, was set on nursing school. They struck a deal with her: if she would stay on an extra year and assume house duties and care for the three youngest children, her father would then take her to his sister in Chicago and help her enroll at Mt. Sinai. Marian's mother (who probably felt she'd earned a break) would go with her middle girls to board in town while they finished high school.

A year later, Mama tried to renegotiate the terms: one more year at home, she argued, and Marian should study to be a teacher. Dan Murphy, who normally surrendered to his wife's every whim, stood firm.

"A promise," he said, "is a promise." My mother-in-law never forgot that her father did the right thing by her, and she never forgot that her mother tried to do her wrong.

Despite her mother's objections, off Marian went to Chicago. She thrived. She studied; she worked; she traveled. She brought brothers and sisters to be educated and paid their way. When war broke out, she signed on with the Navy. She married an Army paratrooper. When they divorced, Marian packed up the two kids and left California. Back in Montana, she raised her son and daughter with an iron hand. They would do well in school, by God. They would be upright, and they would do as they were told. For the most part, they abided by her rules.

But one night, my brave husband Dan slipped out of the house in the middle of the night to party with friends. The next morning, he woke to find his mother standing over the car he'd saved years to buy. She lifted the hood.

"I don't know much about what all this is," she said as she brought up her hammer. "But I am fairly certain I can do some damage." And if he hadn't shaped up, she assuredly would have.

In the years before I knew Marian, she was becoming the person she was when we first met: a woman who cared not a whit for clothes or, actually, things in general. Her passions ran more toward travel and books, particularly Westerns, which she bought at yard or library sales. A dime, she thought, a fair price for a paperback. Wherever Marian went, Louis L'Amour went, too.

She liked Western movies as well, and movies about war. She liked her meat cooked to just this side of jerky. If you put the kettle on and brought the water to a proper boil, she loved a cup of tea. She would sit at the table with a piece of toast and a home canned peach and never need to utter a word. How different she was than we Southern women with our compulsion to fill the very possibility of silence.

Like all the Westerners I've met over time, Marian appreciated a slice of pie, but she couldn't go without potatoes.

"If I don't have a potato every day," she told me as she ate a boiled one, "I feel like I haven't really eaten." That was the Black Irish in her.

And, oh how she loved a game of pinochle.

Dan and I were well into our second decade of marriage when we visited Montana for our niece's wedding. All of the relatives who were currently speaking—those fiery tempers, you know—gathered for a night of cards. The numbers worked out, allowing everyone to participate at tables of four.

"But I don't know how to play," I admitted.

"What?" an adopted aunt exclaimed. "You're married to Dan Lovatt, and you can't play pinochle?"

"That's right," I said. "And what's more, I've never seen him play either."

This revelation dumbfounded the room.

Later I asked Dan privately, "What's up with the cards?"

"When it's 30 degrees outside for months on end, you spend all the time you can inside."

Things Marian didn't like: Jane Fonda topped the list—the mention of her name raised Marion's blood pressure; "the city fathers," as she mockingly called local politicians; injustice. She also abhorred laziness and considered no job gender-specific. Everyone, she believed, should wash and iron and put away clothes. They should know how to iron, clean and change a tire.

Evidently, she'd had her fill of cooking before leaving for Chicago, so if her children wanted something other than frozen vegetables, boiled potatoes, and overdone meat, they were encouraged to hone their skills in the kitchen as well. I have greatly benefitted from this philosophy. Dan braids our granddaughter's hair, sews on buttons, filets, sautés, and makes pickles. Bless you, dear Marian.

Another thing that boiled her blood was the mention of her own mother.

On no account should she be buried by Ma, she told her family. Stanley, the baby, could have that spot. Her final resting place should be on the left side of her father.

Individually and as a group, she told us, "I will not lie for eternity by someone who tried to go back on her word." Those Irish—don't cross them. They know how to bear a grudge.

Although Marian never regretted much that I know of, she did tell me she had been born a little too late.

"I wish I could have been a pioneer," she lamented. "I would have been first in line on the wagon train."

"Really?" I asked. "A pioneer?"

"Oh, yes," she said dreamily. "I would have loved that."

Hmmm, I thought to myself. She must not have seen those movies I grew up with—the ones where women were taken hostage or scalped, men burned alive, death by smallpox, cholera, and typhoid fever. If you didn't die on the trail, you lived in a wagon. Me, I would have been one of those who turned tail and ran back East, but I didn't say so to my mother-in-law.

By that time, I earnestly wished her to think me braver and better in every way than I really was.

Belle Mère: A French Mother-In-Law Story
by Barbara Pasquet James

Anyone who has studied even rudimentary French will instantly recognize that *belle-mère* translates sweetly to, "beautiful mother."

Somewhere along the convoluted path of linguistic evolution—not unlike the gorilla who signed "ice" and "box" to cleverly describe a freezer—these two words magically fused into one concept, and today, belle-mère, incredibly, means "mother-in-law" in French.

Don't get me wrong. A belle-mère *is* a beautiful mother. Indeed. In the glossed-over eyes of her French son, no woman in the world can ever be more beautiful, more seductive—neither wife, daughter, sister, nor mistress—than His Mother.

No female in the universe, no matter how hard she tries, will be able to hold a flame to this woman—whose radiating face he beheld as soon as he emerged into this world. She was the one who bathed him in endless kisses, teased, spoiled, cuddled, praised, and importantly, fed him, day after day, year after year, until he grew into a Man. And oh, what a fine specimen he became.

Laughing at his every quip, funny or not, that was her, quashing squabbles at the dinner table as she took his side against all others, especially Dad, right or wrong. She was the one in the bouncy skirt who'd arrive early at the schoolyard gate, stretching up on tiptoes and upon catching a mere glimpse of his cowlick through a windowpane, smooth her hair, beam, and wave furiously with both arms, as if he were a soldier returning fresh from the battlefield.

Thanks to her, housework would be completely unknown to him. As her *petit chou* pursued the all-revered *baccalaureate*, the French equivalent of an über-high-school diploma, she'd refuse to let such mendacity interfere with his studies.

Every night at dinner, after cajoling him in front of everyone to take that last lamb chop or chicken leg (even though Dad had been eyeing it feverishly), she'd cheerfully clear off the dinner table. It never occurred to her that Son might take his own plate into the kitchen. And, as a grown man, if he drifted off to sleep after a weekend lunch party, snoring away on the couch, she'd smile unapologetically to wincing guests and explain in whispers (so as not to wake him) "he's been working hard" all week. (As if no one else had.)

Yes, from birth to grave and beyond, in France, no woman holds more power over a French son than his Mother. And if she sees herself having to relinquish to something as trivial as the arrival of a Wife on the scene, she will go out of her way to make sure she remains Number One.

Allow me to explain: My mother-in-law is French. But mostly—and this must be kept in mind throughout—first and foremost, she is a French *woman*. Why should that make a difference? Well, it just does.

. Of Austrian and English heritage, Baron Clement von Franckenstein had just completed playing a very convincing (fictional) President of France opposite Michael Douglas and Annette Bening in the blockbuster film *An American President*, beating out eight French actors for the role. Here's what Clement had to say in an interview I did with him that appeared in *Boulevard France*, an international glossy published in London:

"French women love to flirt and tend to immediately think of other women as adversaries. And they don't mind the alienation. Even an unattractive French woman will go out of her way to lure all the men in the room with no apparent sense of self-consciousness. They ignore the other women and make it quite clear what they want. In an acting class situation, it's usually the teacher they go after, and they'll go out of their way to please him, even at the expense of other students, men and women."

Having lived in Paris for years and with French genes from my father's side, I knew that a widely-used seduction technique by many French *femmes* (handed down from grandmother to granddaughter) is to find out what a targeted male likes or admires, then top it.

Here is an example (imagine, please, this dialogue, completely in French):

She (*nonchalante*, blowing smoke straight up into the air): "So tell me, what did you say your favorite color was?"

He (shrugging): "Blue?"

She (crushing out her cigarette, suddenly energized): "*Non! Non non, non!* That cannot be true! Everything in my apartment is blue! La la la! My car, my bathroom wall, even my dishes! It is so weird, isn't it? ISN'T IT INCREDIBLE THAT WE BOTH LOVE BLUE?!!" [Believe it or not I hear this technique works]

Here's another:

He (shrugging): "My dream is to go around the world but..." (His voice trails off as he looks hopelessly into the far distance).

She (crushing out her cigarette, suddenly energized): "Don't tell me! I had a dream, so real, that I was on a boat, with someone, but who? I couldn't make out his face! We stopped at many exotic places, so far away, and it was oh so romantic." (A boat trip around the world seems to be the SFMD, Standard French Male Dream).

He (incredulous): "Don't tell me!"

So I suppose that is why, whenever we'd visit my parents-in-law in the countryside and go out to eat, a tiny flag would spring up every time Mother-In-Law went out of her way to order exactly whatever my husband did, no matter what was being ordered by everyone else.

The first few times this happened, I thought I was being overly-sensitive. A gut feeling told me she was just trying to please, and what's wrong with that? But the Woman side of me recalled how she ran to put on lipstick whenever she heard his car roll up in the driveway.

Once, when he'd nipped out to pick up an extra *baguette*, my mother-in-law noticed that I had caught her primping. She tossed her hair back in glee like a young girl, laughing it off.

"*Mon dieu*, you never had a son, so how could you possibly understand?" She made a mad sprint for the door.

When the four of us (parents-in-law, my husband, and myself) go to a restaurant, out of *politesse*, we *femmes* are deferred to and order first. Usually, I know what I want. Then I order, and it's her turn. Predictably, she'll say she hasn't decided and then turn to Son to find out what *he's* having.

If he says he'll go for the *confit de canard* (preserved duck), she'll slam her menu shut and gush, "*Incroyable!* I'll have that, too! We always choose the same things!"

Never mind that father-in-law is quietly glaring at the menu over his glasses, brow twisted in pain as he contemplates such uncharacteristic enthusiasm in his otherwise composed spouse.

If my husband says he's not very hungry, neither is she. If he says he doesn't like something, she loathes it. If he orders something I don't much care for such as say, tongue, she'll lean back in her chair and, looking perplexed, reflect out loud, "It is strange that Bah-bah-rah does not like tongue, non?" searching faces for support. "How can Bah-bah-rah not like tongue?!"

Conclusion: "Bah-bah-rah is not like us!"

Thus, having my incongruity publicly aired and my name turned into three syllables, I smile uncomfortably while my husband takes in her comments with his usual good humor.

That is why one evening, after father-in-law suggested we meet up at a Vietnamese restaurant in a nearby village, I took it upon myself to mention the, "I'll-have-whatever-he's-having" behavior during the drive over.

My husband was stunned.

No. He was *angry*.

Didn't I know what I was implying? That my belle-mère—His Mother!—was practically flirting with her own son? Oh, insidious Oedipal connotations! What a horrid thing to say!

I slunk down in my seat.

"So what if she were?" I fought back after giving it some thought "*Mamista*," I reminded him, "was very much alive, much more flagrant, and totally accepted over the not-too-distant Italian border."

I pointed out that millions of full-grown Italian men with families of their own were joyfully transporting bags of soiled laundry, often traveling great distances, to grateful *Mamas* to wash and fold, even as we spoke.

But it was hopeless. We drove on in silence.

The restaurant overlooked a small square with a fountain. Inside, wafts of garlic mixed with sounds of chatter and laughter. We took our seats, and immediately, *les cartes* were placed before us. I was drawn to prawns encrusted in salt and pepper but decided to hang back and see what everyone else was having.

While waiting, father-in-law suggested we start with a platter of *nems*, small crispy spring rolls made with rice paper, to which everyone heartily agreed. Good start.

Meanwhile, Mother-In-Law studied the menu carefully. Then, without looking up, demurely, (and in a noticeably higher-than-usual voice), asked my husband, "*Cheri*, and what are you having?"

"Beef with basil," he said, slowly turning the page to peruse the wine list.

That was it. Upon hearing his choice she sat erect, tossed her menu to one side and, spreading her fingers on the table declared, "I'm definitely having what he's having!"

The waiter arrived to take our orders.

I went first. "Salt and pepper encrusted prawns please."

Then it was her turn.

"Beef with basil!" Her lips pursed in triumph as she picked up her menu and shoved it at the waiter, beaming at Son with wide eyes that said, "There!"

My husband: "Beef with basil."

Now in a state of raptured satisfaction, she ignored both me and my father-in-law, whose chin was settled in resignation in both palms. As the twinkle in her eye twinkled, father-in-law let out a huge French sigh, the kind of sigh that sounds like air slowly seeping out of a flattening tire.

Then the silence broke.

"I adore basil. I love it!" she said, strumming her fingers on the tabletop.

No one responded.

"And what about you. Do you like basil, Bah-bah-rah?" she asked me, with a disarmingly friendly grin.

The waiter waited and looked slightly bemused.

"Yes, very much." I was surprised she cared.

"Well, I like it more than you possibly ever could. Did you know that I dreamed of basil just the other night?"

No, I didn't.

"Yes, I did. It was an extraordinary dream. That odor, that wonderful basil odor, was everywhere." She rolled her eyes heavenward in ecstasy, then, rolling them down again, fixed them firmly on Son and continued, "And then, I passed myself in a mirror and poof! I WAS ENVELOPED IN BASIL. I had actually turned into, well, basil!"

"Monsieur?" my husband broke in. Everyone turned to look at him. His brow was knit, and something on the menu seemed to have nabbed his gaze.

Belle-mère cocked her head sharply to one side. She looked

confused. Irritated. He'd already decided, hadn't he? What could he possibly be doing?

"I changed my mind. I'll have the duck with pineapple," my husband said, handing his menu to the waiter, who nodded, and scribbled it down.

Father-in-law smiled. "Make that two."

Belle-mère struggled to grab the carte, but father-in-law snapped it away and patted her hand. "There, there my dear. You dreamed of basil. It was an extraordinary dream. And so real. You became basil, did you not? The odors were wonderful. So now, just be happy with what you're getting!"

His Mother was My Mom

by Lois Rauch Gibson

My mother-in-law, Eleanor J. Gibson, died in December 2002, and I still miss her, especially when I am cooking or trying to complete a *New York Times* double-crostic puzzle. We had a warm and loving relationship, lived together part of each year for over a decade, shared interests and tastes, and respected each other.

Those ages-old, awful, mother-in-law jokes never applied to us. Ours was not a sit-com relationship. Yet people kept saying I deserved a halo for living with *his* mother. Even when I insisted that I not only loved but also liked my mother-in-law, the raised eyebrows and skeptical looks continued. For all of those jaded folks, our story provides proof that a positive mother-in-law/daughter-in-law relationship can exist.

For many years after she retired from being a full-time professor of psychology, my mother-in-law was what we in the South call a "snow-bird." She spent summers in her house in Vermont, near her daughter, and lived with my husband and me in our South Carolina home from October through May.

This arrangement suited all of us, partly because my mother-in-law was really my mother. Even when she was in Vermont, we called each other often to compare answers to the *New York Times* crossword puzzle, and to share recipes and reactions to books. Well into her eighties, she learned to use the Internet, and we also emailed.

She proved to be a wonderful resource for my children as they grew up. Not only did they have a live-in grandma to whom they felt very close, but she was also a role model they watched grow older but remain productive professionally. She served as a great idea bank for science projects, too, having shepherded many graduate students through psychology experiments. She also did more than her share of cooking.

Under her influence, we ate family dinners, despite soccer, band practice, karate, and countless other interferences. My sons complained that we were the only family they knew who ate dinner together in the dining room, without any mustard or ketchup bottles on the table (Grandma's rule), and had conversations. They complained, but they loved it. She was an integral part of our lives, and we loved our old-fashioned, three-generation household.

Mom and I were not always that close, but I think we always liked each other—something of a surprise to me, since I expected to be over-awed by her before I met her. When I first met her son Jerry in 1967, he told me his parents were psychologists at Cornell, and I actually remembered his mom's famous "visual cliff" experiments—the one everyone who ever took Introduction to Psychology remembers: all the texts have that cute picture of a kitten or baby goat or human infant on a glass platform, with a checkered tablecloth under the glass. The experiments demonstrated that an animal able to navigate has depth perception and will not deliberately walk over the edge of a table or cliff. The research fascinated me, and I was impressed to discover that I was dating Eleanor J. Gibson's son.

Shortly after New Year's Day in 1969, Jerry and I went skiing in Vermont and planned to stop in Ithaca, New York, to visit his parents on the way back to Pittsburgh, where he attended medical school, and I worked toward a Ph.D. in English. The night we left Vermont was cold and snowy. I had a sore throat, stuffed head, muscle aches—a full-blown cold. Jerry drove an ancient station wagon that had once belonged to his parents. Before long, the snow became a blizzard, and the New York State Thruway closed. We had to drive through silent, snow-covered small towns with narrow streets and nothing moving except the snowflakes and us.

My cold worsened, visibility was nearly zero, and the gas needle pointed ominously toward empty.

"Why don't we just find a motel and call your mother to explain. Surely, she'd want to hear we're doing the sensible thing," I suggested. "Besides, I don't want to arrive at three or four in the morning, especially not with this cold."

"Mom will be up. She's always up reading," he insisted. "Both of my parents are night people," he claimed. "Besides, where would we find a motel on these back roads?"

And so we continued on with the gas gauge relentlessly pressing toward empty, and all the gas stations we passed along the way closed.

Finally, we stopped at one of the stations, hoping without reason that the owner was nearby. To our amazement, a police officer in a cruiser miraculously materialized with a key to the gas pump. I felt a little relieved that at least we wouldn't be lost, gasless, in a snow drift along the way.

Many snowy roads later, we arrived at "111 Oak Hill Road," as friends always affectionately called the Gibson home. As Jerry had predicted, the lights blazed, and his mother came to the door with a book in her hand—*Pride and Prejudice!*—which she said she was reading *again*.

Anyone who loved Jane Austen *had* to be a kindred spirit, I thought and relaxed a bit. Years later, Mom said she had, of course, been worried about us that night. Unlike her husband, who worked all night in his study, she was a morning person, but her anxiety had kept her awake. That's why she had been reading Austen.

Coincidentally, when reading an early draft of this essay, my younger son smiled and said, "You do that too!" And he's right: I often resorted to a favorite author—sometimes even Austen— when my grown children arrived later than expected.

Later that same week of the snowstorm in 1969, as Jerry and I prepared to leave for Pittsburgh, his mother said, "Can't you stay one more day? Jerry hasn't had any mince pie yet, and I was going to bake one today."

So, I thought, she uses the guilt card, too. It was something I had naively assumed belonged to the stereotypical Jewish mother. I was charmed.

Mom claimed it helps if a mother-in-law and daughter-in-law have something in common, as she and I did, yet she and her mother-in-law built a comfortable, if not close, relationship with little in common but the grandchildren. And if Mom and I judged by our family histories, we should have had little in common.

Her Scotch Irish Presbyterian ancestors have been in this country since the 1630s; my Eastern European Jewish grandparents arrived at the onset of the 20th century. Branches of her family tree include colonial ministers, distinguished Revolutionary and Civil War officers, and some illustrious members of the Hooker family—founders of Connecticut. Rev. Lyman Beecher's daughter Isabella married a later Hooker, named John; Mom's mother, Isabel Hooker Grier, was named for her and received a copy of *Uncle Tom's Cabin* from Isabella's sister Harriet, inscribed, "To little Isabel...from Harriet Beecher Stowe."

In contrast, my family fled the czar; one grandfather was a tailor who made fancy clothes and buttons for soldiers and rich civilians in Warsaw. Other ancestors were peasants and workers, though students of the Torah.

But both Mom's ancestors and mine came to America seeking religious freedom though they came from different circumstances and social classes in both the Old World and the New. Her mother attended college, and their family had a live-in cook. My generation was the first in our family to attend college; not all of my parents' siblings even completed high school because they needed to work to help support the family.

One amusing cultural difference between our families involved alcohol. My family served kosher wine ceremoniously, but I found it unpleasantly sweet. Sometimes my grandmother added a bit to seltzer to make a slightly flavored drink, but I did not like that either. Hardly anyone drank any other alcohol. I vaguely remember whispered remarks about my grandfather's occasional glass of *schnapps*, a potent European brandy. But mostly, I recall my mother's horror when the doctor suggested that my father have one drink each evening to help lower his blood pressure: she considered this tantamount to alcoholism.

In contrast, my mother-in-law's family served evening cocktails and held parties at which drinks were served. According to a family story shared with me (which Mom claims her younger sister fabricated) Mom and her cousin Cassie at about age eleven went around after one party tasting the dregs of each guest's drink. Maybe it never happened, but in my family, it never *could* have happened.

During my first visit to 111 Oak Hill Road, I learned about the Sidecar, a drink Jerry's dad always mixed for guests, with nearly equal parts of triple sec, brandy, and lemon juice. He claimed the fruit made it very healthy. But he never warned me it could be sneakily intoxicating. I had only one Sidecar, and then I asked if I could help with dinner.

"Mmmm, well, you could set the table," Mom said.

I stared blankly at the knives, forks, and spoons, knowing certain etiquette rules dictated their placement. Even in my plebian home I had learned that—but that Sidecar had apparently numbed my brain. I simply couldn't remember.

Embarrassed, I placed utensils and napkins on the table and hoped no one would notice if anything was out of place. And apparently no one did. Years later, I was the only one who remembered what I had thought of then as a humiliating event.

Throughout our life together, though, Mom and I had very different drinking habits. We both enjoyed wine with dinner, but

I drank one glass—or none if I planned to grade papers later. We often joked that one bottle of Scotch could last me several years. Mom, on the other hand, drank several glasses of vodka and water on ice with a bit of lemon peel every evening while watching the news on public television before dinner. She bought vodka often enough that the woman who manages the local liquor store knew her name and preferences.

One early autumn day, before Mom returned for the winter, I stopped in to buy vermouth and sherry for cooking. "Where's Mama?!" the manager exclaimed.

Nobody in a liquor store had ever recognized me before! But since Mom's death, this kind woman speaks lovingly of her each time I stop by, and tells me what a good daughter I was.

Despite our very different backgrounds, Mom and I reached across the generations and the differences to build a loving, mutually enriching relationship. With help from my brother-in-law (who is also Jewish), I taught Mom to enjoy Passover Seders and Chanukah candles. I learned from her to put oranges in the toes of Christmas stockings and to safeguard the Christmas tree skirt embroidered by her, Aunt Emily, my sister-in-law Jean, and me.

Mom participated in the bar mitzvah ceremonies of my sons and helped me bake *ruggalach* (a traditional pastry) from my grandmother's recipe, and I have made Christmas pudding and cookies. I attended Friends' Meetings with Mom and Jean in Vermont, and with Mom in South Carolina, where we all felt spiritually and emotionally comfortable.

Aside from Jane Austen and academia, Mom and I shared recipes and mystery novels. We both hated to shop for clothing, but we enjoyed planning and shopping for meals. We loved *Jane Eyre*; biographies of interesting, successful women; and simple, comfortable clothing. We even used the same cures for insomnia, as we discovered once in Oregon while crossing the Columbia River.

"Oh, this is one of my favorite rivers beginning with the letter 'c'!" Mom said.

Instantly and eagerly, we compared notes on how we both go through the alphabet, naming rivers, cities, mountains, or whatever comes to mind, to help us fall asleep.

We also helped with each other's work. When she felt ill and unable to review abstracts submitted to a colloquium, I read them aloud to her. We laughed at how often she voted thumbs down on papers I had secretly considered hopelessly boring or pedantic.

When I taught children's literature in Oregon, Mom came to my classes to discuss fairy tales; when she co-taught a freshman seminar on fairy tales at Middlebury College, I helped her respond to students' papers. We often read and commented on each other's manuscripts, including this one, which I completed in draft form before she died. I found her advice sound and remarkably tactful for one who stated that among the few advantages of growing old is the freedom to speak bluntly.

For much of my life, I envied girls who had close relationships with their mothers. I found among these women several temporary surrogate mothers, but I yearned for one of my own. My mother, a troubled woman, took care of me and no doubt loved me, but she was not able to get close to anyone or to express love. As a child, I felt cheated.

Later, I realized my mother gave me what she could. Her mother and sisters tried to fill the gap a bit, but the absence of a nurturing mother hurt. My mother-in-law filled that gap and became a role model for me.

Mom also maintained a close bond with her daughter Jean and with many graduate students who saw her as more than just their intellectual mentor. One of them professed shock to discover that she knew Jackie (my mother-in-law's nickname) better than she knew her own mother. She even knew about Jackie's favorite tea and cocktail. And before she married, her prospective husband had to gain Jackie's approval.

Many of Mom's former grad students have similar stories to tell about her professional and personal mentoring, and they told them amidst tears and laughter at the memorial events we held for her, with vodka and Sidecars for all. One grad student even named her daughter Eleanor.

When my first child was born, my in-laws came to help. They cooked, ran errands, changed diapers, and "taught" Michael Stephen (as my father-in-law loved to call him) baby tricks. They did insist we change the spelling of his middle name to the British *Stephen*, after we had opted for the easier-to-spell *Steven*, but that seemed minor then and now—humorous rather than annoying. They babysat on our wooden deck in the glorious warmth of a sunny Portland, Oregon, August day, while we went off to change the birth certificate.

When I worried about making the right decisions in raising my children, Mom told me to make sure they always knew I loved them, and the rest would fall into place.

And as a mother of young children, I once told Mom that her success made me feel inadequate—that I could never hope to be as professionally productive as she had been. She responded simply, "You're a good mother and a good teacher, and if you chose to do research later, there will be time."

She had long ago decided that a woman could choose two of the three areas to do well. Her circumstances led her to be a mother and a researcher first. She married psychologist James J. Gibson in the era when nepotism rules worked mostly against women. When they moved to Cornell, his faculty status denied her a position for sixteen years and forced her to find her own research grants. She trained many graduate students on those grants, and they became another sort of Gibson offspring, many of them attending a celebration of her achievements when she "retired" at Cornell.

I use quotation marks around the word retired because Eleanor Gibson never retired. In the 1980s and already in her seventies, she held a position as Visiting Professor at Emory University and guided two graduate students through experimental research to doctorates. Then, despite a heart valve replacement and bouts with pneumonia, cancer, and heart disease, she continued to write.

In 1999, nearly 89 years old, she completed (with Anne Pick, another former student who is now retired and a grandmother herself) an up-to-date text on perceptual development. At the suggestion of her family, she then began a memoir of herself and her husband, *Perceiving the Affordances: A Memoir of Two Psychologists*, which was published in 2002. She urged her grandchildren to find careers they could love and find fulfilling throughout life.

Certainly she did so. She worked until her death, even leaving
behind an incomplete draft of a murder mystery set in a
psychology department.

When Mom read a draft of this manuscript about her, she
worried first that I had made her sound like an alcoholic (I assured
her no one would think that!) and second, she felt I presented too
idealized a picture of her. So I include here a conflict of which she
was unaware until I wrote it down.

In February 1981, Mom stayed with my two-week old son
Jonathan while I went a few miles away to present a paper at a
statewide conference. Perhaps that's why she and Jerry thought I
was ready for a trip to find a beach house to buy on the South
Carolina coast.

But actually, I was exhausted and unenthusiastic. With two
small children and a job to which I would soon return, the last
thing I wanted was more responsibility. I thought Mom would
understand. Yet she seemed to think I was being difficult. Already
moody and miserable, I gave in.

Off we went to the coast, from realtor to realtor, house to
house. When Jonathan began spitting up immediately after
nursing that first night, I thought at first he was sick. Then I feared
my own tension caused his upset. And on top of that, it seemed
to me that Jerry and Mom felt I deliberately tried to delay seeing
realtors.

I sat on the worn sofa in the rented beach house feeling
drained, frightened, angry, and guilty—a horrible experience. It
turned out that Jonathan, born three weeks early, had an immature
esophageal sphincter, a condition that caused his spitting up and
resolved itself in time.

Mom and Jerry eventually built a beach house at Fripp Island. She often vacationed there with us and sometimes wrote papers there with former grad students. Mom always loved the house, and in time, I, too, grew to love it. So even that misunderstanding eventually worked itself out.

Over time, our relationship grew overwhelmingly positive. With mutual respect and support, we benefited, I hope, equally. Mom was grateful for all I did for her as she grew older, especially during her many bouts with illness and declining health. Sometimes I slept on a sofa outside her room, or in a chair in her hospital room. Sleeping anywhere else, worry would have kept me from sleeping at all.

And Mom cared for me, too, when I was very ill with chicken pox in Switzerland in 1989. I had long wanted to hear her give a lecture in her field, and I had planned to hear her speak to psychologists at the University of Geneva (in English, but answering questions in French). But the day of the lecture, I became so sick with *la varicella*, I actually blacked out. I awoke with my eleven-year-old son—who also had chicken pox—anxiously watching over me.

Several days later, my husband flew off to Africa. I threatened to divorce him if he left me alone with chicken pox, but he calmly pointed out that Mom was there—as she was. She shopped for groceries, cooked for us in our tiny apartment, made sure the children got off to school (once they were healthy), went over homework, and tried to make me comfortable—no easy task.

Shortly before she left for the United States, I recovered enough to drive across the border to Divonne les Bains with her to spend her remaining French francs on souvenirs, food, and lunch. After buying a soup cookbook for her daughter, plus the two liters of wine and one kilo of meat we were allowed to take back into Switzerland, Mom still had what seemed like a huge number of francs, and we were hungry. I spied workers heading for a small restaurant and suggested we eat there because I had discovered that workers generally choose places that serve hearty local fare. But Mom demurred.

"Didn't I see a sign for some place with a Michelin rating?" she asked. "I think it was a *château* with at least one star," she added. (The Michelin Red Guide is one of Europe's oldest hotel and restaurant reference guides, which awards *Michelin stars* to rate these establishments.)

I looked at our damp raincoats and soggy shoes and pictured Michelin patrons and prices.

"Oh, come on! Let's look for it," she urged. "You need a treat. We should celebrate your recovery!"

So off we went to the *Château de Divonne*, high on a hill overlooking Geneva. What an experience! From the moment we entered, tradition and elegance surrounded us. A dignified host ushered us to a tiny round table in a small room, where a second took our droopy, cloth raincoats. A third host handed us wine menus to peruse as we awaited our table. A fourth escorted us to a table for two in a small dining room which held no more than six tables, only two of them occupied. A fifth brought us menus and took our orders, while a bread waiter and a wine waiter hovered nearby. (More waiters than patrons!—this was a novelty for me.")

But ordering provided a challenge. Determined not to use credit cards and to limit our spending to what no longer seemed an enormous number of francs, Mom and I decided on one main dish and one glass of wine each, selecting different dishes and wines, so we could sample each other's fare.

All food was *a la carte*, so we did not get to sample soup or salad, but a wonderful little *terrine* did appear with the bread. The food was excellent if not abundant, and the service was embarrassingly solicitous. In the unquestionably elegant ambience, we noticed the wallpaper even matched the china. Limoges? We wondered. To Mom's horror (and amusement), I surreptitiously raised a plate to look, and, of course, it was Limoges.

With Mom's francs and a few from my purse, we barely covered the bill. Later, I told a British friend living in Divonne where we had lunched, and she gasped. "You actually *ate* there? Everyone we know just goes there to sit on the terrace with a drink and enjoy the view."

And even though Mom and I had a view obscured by clouds and rain, we felt we'd gotten our money's worth and much amusement for years to come as we recalled the adventure of the Michelin star lunch, which never would have happened if Mom had not insisted on a fitting celebration of my triumph over chicken pox.

Of course, her insistence on the Michelin over the workers' choice for lunch also highlights her tendency to be more elitist than I am. Sometimes I bristled at her elitism, aware of my own roots. When she read this comment, Mom, a longtime liberal, was not pleased. But when we did crossword puzzles together, she took pride in not knowing the names of television shows, baseball players, or popular singers and grew irritated when clues asked for such information. She scorned popular culture and expressed amazement when I knew, for example, that a hockey great is nearly always Orr, and an actress named Hatcher or Garr is Teri.

"How on earth would you know a thing like that?" she would exclaim. She also dismissed most newspapers other than the *Times* as worthless and watched no television except PBS.

All relationships take work, but living with another human being takes more. Certainly, my mother-in-law and I worked at our relationship. If anything, we each tried too hard to do what we thought the other preferred. Mom constantly apologized, often for no reason: "I'm sorry. I'm just sitting down because I feel tired."

"It's all right, Mom," I would reply, "You have a perfect right to sit. Please don't apologize."

"Oh, I beg your pardon," she'd respond—and then laugh, realizing she had just apologized for apologizing. We had that very exchange many times, and I found if I did not laugh also, I became exasperated. So I learned to laugh.

But this attempt to accommodate at times led to misunderstanding and confusion, such as the time I came home to find Mom baking salmon covered in foil.

"Oh," I said, interested, "I usually broil it."

Thinking my remark critical rather than curious, Mom became defensive. Then she apologized for "doing it the wrong way." And I became defensive and tried to explain what I meant. We went round and round in increasingly tense circles. Then we stopped and hugged.

Hugging is part of who I am—a traditional hugger. Though my mother was not good at this, my dad was, and later in life, my grandmother liked hugging, too. But I learned early in our relationship that hugs made Mom uncomfortable, so I gradually, reluctantly, learned to hold back. Then as she grew older, mom wanted to be hugged! So I gladly reverted to my norm. During her final hospital stay, we hugged often, both of us knowing the end was near.

On her 92nd birthday, just weeks before she died, she told me she had lived long enough.

"I know I promised to help you," I said, "but physician-assisted suicide is legal only in Oregon. Should I get us tickets to stay with Michael in Portland?" (My older son had returned to the city where he was born to attend law school in the very neighborhood where Mom and Dad babysat him that warm August day when Jerry and I went off to correct his birth certificate.)

Mom smiled and remained silent.

She spoke often in the last months of being ready to die. Once when I jokingly told her I was too busy for that and asked her to wait, she asked, "Well, when *will* you have time?"

"During my summer vacation," I smiled teasingly.

Mom, fiercely independent as always, died during winter vacation, and I was with her every day at the end.

Despite all the mother-in-law jokes and horror stories one hears, I know I am not the only woman who cherishes my relationship with my husband's mother. In 1996, I attended a Hunter College High School reunion. Though now co-ed, Hunter operated as a school for "intellectually gifted girls" in my day.

At the reunion class lunch, each woman present was asked to share something of significance that had happened to us in the decades since high school. We were a successful group, yet among the comments by lawyers, professors, physicians, performers, teachers, political appointees, college administrators, at least one best-selling author, and so on, the words I remember had nothing to do with careers.

One classmate stood up and announced, "I have been married three times, and I have three wonderful mothers-in-law!" Though no longer married to their sons, she remained in contact with their mothers. They were her friends, family, and comrades for life.

I have been married only once, and I had only one mother-in-law—a wonderful one, at that, and our relationship clearly demonstrates that it need not take a halo for a daughter-in-law and mother-in-law to build a strong relationship. It takes only love and respect and determination.

My mother-in-law and I shared all three.

Family Time
by Margaret Bell

"Wild Time"

My in-laws gave me a birthday present that looked like a tired brown squirrel splayed across the marble of their coffee table. Glitter from the package's ribbon sprinkled the fuzzy lump, like shiny dandruff.

Margaret, the new wife of my new husband's father, leaned toward me. "Here, let me help you put it on." She spoke loudly above Goldie Hawn telling us to "Sock it to me" as Laugh-In played on the big console across the room. Margaret picked up the hair piece and began to attach it to my head.

"I think the color is just right for your skin tone," she mumbled with a mouth full of bobby pins. Her red satin hot pants brushed against my jeans. Her silver, halter held breasts of wonder.

On the other side of the table, my new husband Richard leaned toward his father to tell him, "Dad, you need to lick the paper more to get a better seal."

Richard's father fumbled with the joint and then shoved it toward his son.

"Damn it, you do it." He laughed and took a gulp from his engraved high-ball glass, as slivers of grass fell into the thick shag carpet. "Seems like a lot of trouble just to get a little buzz."

My father-in-law had the idea to try marijuana for his first time that night, so he asked Richard to bring some to my birthday dinner. "So I can see what the hell Walter Cronkite talks about so much."

But the preparations proved frustrating to him.

"Margaret, better open that other bottle. I think we're going to need it."

Of course, he didn't really need any more recreational substances, since his daily fifth of bourbon cushioned him fine. It kept him mostly mellow and functioning as well as his recent retirement schedule required. He no longer went into his insurance company office to work. Instead, he wrote investment checks to new friends with plans for shopping malls or ski resorts in the middle of the Kansas plains. If given enough drinks at the fancy clubs he attended, his check book opened easily. He had met Margaret at one of those clubs. She was a friend of a friend twice removed, twenty years younger, and recently divorced.

The previous year, Richard's mother, Kathryn, had died from a sudden illness. Richard came home from Basic Training to attend her funeral. He and I were not yet engaged, and to my regret, I had not known her well. We only knew each other through her only child. She loved him, and so did I.

As I sat quietly with the dead squirrel on my head and fingered the pattern on my in-law's new brocade couch, I looked for signs of Kathryn at this party. She had not lived in this fancy new house, so the only remnant I found of her was a cherry bookcase in the corner that Richard told me once held her books. Now it was piled with a slippery stack of magazines.

"Margaret, damn it, my drink is empty."

My head jerked up at the shout of my name from Richard's father. Then I remembered that his new wife and I shared the same name. It felt a little crowded to have another Margaret Bell in the room. I wondered if Richard would be upset if I changed back to my maiden name.

"Just you settle down, Mr. Bell. Your waitress is busy in the kitchen right now," Margaret joked with him as she got a bowl of salad from the refrigerator. I did a double-take as she added with a serious face, "You just suck on your ice cubes for a minute, 'cause I'm not giving you any more ice. Too much ice isn't good for your health."

"Son, women are getting mighty uppity these days."

Richard didn't joke back at his father's words. Instead he carried his father's glass to the kitchen for a refill. As he walked by me, he pointed to his watch and mouthed, "We can leave right after dinner."

I got up to help Margaret set the table. I walked slowly with a stiff neck, balancing the squirrel on my head. With each step, more glitter drifted down, frosting the screen-printed image of Gloria Steinem on my t-shirt.

"Grace Time"

When the money ran out, Margaret did the sensible thing. She took to her bed.

A few days later, Richard's father called to ask us to help her pack up their house. He explained, "She needs some extra hands, but I'm no good at that kind of thing. Besides, I'm meeting my banker at the club to get this mess straightened out."

Richard hung up the phone slowly and looked over at me eavesdropping nearby.

"What does he mean, he's 'no good at that kind of thing'?" My voice got louder. "Sticking stuff in boxes is not complicated."

It rose even more. "Of course, explaining the mistakes to Margaret could be messy, particularly since he caused the problems himself." I could easily have railed on more.

Then Richard pitched his voice much lower than mine to say, "You are totally right." At that point, I was certain I'd married a smart and clever man.

At my in-law's house, the eviction notice pinned on the outside of the door fluttered in the breeze while we waited on the porch.

"Thanks for coming by," Margaret said when she answered the doorbell. She gestured toward the notice. "I thought that might get your Dad's attention." She shrugged, "But he seems to think he can talk his way out of debt."

Once in the house, she gestured for us to sit on the brocade couch. "Can I get you some coffee?"

I smiled and shook my head. Richard said, "No, thanks, we're fine. Just show us the boxes, and we'll get started with the packing."

Margaret answered, "No, I'm good with that. Packing's not a big deal. I just wanted to talk with someone. Seems like all our friends are simultaneously unavailable." She said this casually, as if remarking on yesterday's weather.

Richard sighed. He clearly preferred cleaning out the garage to talking about his father. He fiddled with a tissue to clean his glasses, waiting for someone in the room to change the subject.

I practiced how to be a good wife and helped him out. "This change must come as a surprise to you," I said to Margaret. And that was all it took.

She cuddled the silk pillow from her chair and stretched her legs to the footstool. Then Margaret told us more about herself, her other husbands and rough times, her near-by sons, and her little farmhouse outside of town.

She wrapped up by saying, "I got to tell you, I was hoping this was going to work out."

When she said 'this', she gestured toward the big room. She then joked, "It's more fun to be rich than hustle good drinks for bad tips."

Richard and I had a lot of questions, but left them all unasked. Instead, Richard leaned toward her.

"We wish it could have been different. But I know even less than you do about my Dad's money deals." He glanced toward me. "Dad and I are good at arguing politics, but that's about all the talking we do."

Margaret smiled, "Yeah, I kind of figured that. Look, don't you guys worry too much. We'll be fine. I've still got my house out on Route Fifteen. We'll move all this nice stuff to the country, and when you come back to Kansas to visit, we'll be there." Margaret knew we would soon be moving a thousand miles away to graduate school.

Richard still fidgeted on the couch. "Seriously, Margaret, I'd feel a lot better if we did at least a little work while we're here."

"Well, then, come on into the kitchen. You can clean out all the bottom cabinets. If sweating makes you feel better, you're going to feel just fine."

We laughed together and headed for the kitchen. As I passed her, I put my hand on hers. "I wish we'd had more time to get to know each other."

She hugged me. "It's fun sharing a name with you."

She moved away, but then turned back to ask me, "By the way, how come you're not wearing your hair piece today?"

Then she smiled.

"End Time"

When we brought our kids to their grandfather's funeral, they played with Lego's next to his casket. There were no visitors, no bent knees, no organ music, no receiving lines. Just a coffin, us, and Margaret.

Margaret's tears were shed earlier, in spurts over the years. Although frequently interrupted by the drama of her husband's alcoholic excesses, she had cobbled together a life.

In her call to Richard from outside the ICU, she cried that the hospital could not stop his father's internal bleeding. His liver was rock solid from cirrhosis.

"I told him and told him that so much ice was going to kill him," she sobbed. Richard and I never understood if her toxic ice cube theory was real for her, or just a euphemism that enabled her to not smash his bourbon bottles in fury.

Years before this last call, at the start of the End Time, we had arranged with Margaret that if she needed money to run their household, she should call us collect. She used this help only occasionally, and then it was always for a specific problem.

"Richard, I'm sorry to ask, but we got another notice from the power company." We always sent our contributions to Margaret directly, in flowery cards from me to her. If his dad saw Richard's handwriting, he'd fuss to open the envelope himself and the money ended up in his pocket, instead of spent where Margaret most needed it.

After the burial, Richard and I and the kids went back to Margaret's farmhouse. We used the back door since the boards of the front porch were loose and rotted through.

"We've had so much rain this year," Margaret explained.

In the living room, their brocade couch had a painter's plastic tarp draped over it. The dining room table held buckets to catch drops from the leaky roof. A plastic dishpan with an inch of murky water in it sat on the top shelf of Richard's mother's bookcase.

Margaret boiled hot dogs for our lunch and spread a blanket on the living room floor. The kids enjoyed the fun of Margaret's indoor picnic. Our daughter took charge of the ketchup bottle and squeezed too much for all of us. As we laughed, Richard handed Margaret a check for the funeral costs. She tucked it into her bra.

"I guess I won't need to use my private safety deposit box anymore." She smiled as she wiped our son's messy chin.

Then she brought out a shoe box crammed with papers. In a serious voice, she told us, "You might want to look at our bank records, just so you know there's no inheritance for you guys."

Richard shook his head. "We don't need to see them. We just want to double-check that you'll be all right for the future."

Margaret nodded. "I'll be more than fine. With your Dad's social security and that insurance policy we kept up over the years, I'll even be able to get my little house patched up. My boys are nearby, and they'll help with that."

"It doesn't feel right to be better off because he's gone." She sounded sad as she scooped papers back into the shoe box. When she came to a large card stuck in with the bank papers, she smiled slightly and handed it to us.

Scrolls of roses decorated the front of the card. The message inside read 'To the best mother-in-law ever', with pink rosebuds scattered above my signature. She shook her head slowly. "I remember when you sent the last check in this card. I swear, I was sure we were going to have our electric shut off."

We soon started to clean up from our lunch. As we put our plates in the kitchen sink, Margaret took the card from her pocket and put it on the refrigerator.

Then we said our goodbyes and headed to the airport for our flight home.

A Price Above Rubies
by Bobbi Adams

I n my mind's eye, she sits on the couch in the den of the family home, in shorts, fingernails and toenails bright red, a cigarette between her fingers—Betty Gerald McCutchen Austin (1915-1985), middle daughter of a rural physician, mother, mother-in-law.

Introductions between us were made by her childhood friend with whom I cycled this small rural South Carolina town every evening. At the time, I lived in the rear apartment of an antebellum mansion next door to the home where Betty raised her three children. My future husband was her middle child.

The family called Betty and her two sisters the three graces— Betty the most down to earth member of this trio. She mopped her own kitchen floor and mowed her own grass, yet remained a southern lady. She worked outside the home, first in the office of one of the town's lawyers and, much later, as church secretary.

Social and religious life revolved around the Bishopville Presbyterian Church. As her three children grew to high school and college age, Betty assumed more responsibilities in church life. In 1949, she was listed as treasurer of Women of the Church. In 1955, she chaired the Bradley Circle and later the Gregg Circle.

Lightning hit the church in 1966 knocking a piece of stoneware coping through the choir loft's stained glass window of cherub angels. According to a history of the Bishopville Presbyterian Church written for its 150th anniversary, page 34, the following was recorded: "Through the kindness of Mrs. H.C. Austin, a few pieces of the window were collected for the colors and a picture of the three cherubs sketched for the [glass] artist. The window was reproduced, but when first installed the cherubs were up-side down. Three times the glass company made adjustments. Mrs. Austin commented, 'Just how many ways can one turn a picture?'"

She became president of the women of the church, and shortly before her death in 1985, Betty Gerald McCutchen Austin became the first female deacon of the church. I attended the ceremony in which she was installed in 1983, and I saw great humility as she knelt in front of the church upon her election.

She most loved her three children and two grandchildren. Sundays everyone gathered for a noontime meal around the oak claw foot table in the middle of the kitchen. I often manned the kitchen to finish up some of the meals while Betty was at church and my husband, his father, and two nephews went arrowhead hunting on Indian mounds in the county.

On any given Sunday, the menu might include New England pot pie, red chicken stew, spare ribs, or shrimp and red rice. Sides included sweet potatoes prepared with brown sugar and smothered with pecans, curried fruit, and slaw made with vinegar, not mayonnaise. This recipe took an entire cabbage, cut with a knife, not grated. Dessert was often fruit pie or chess pie. Butter cream icing on white cake was also a favorite.

A family Christmas with all her children, her husband, grandchildren, and out-laws like me, heralded the season with Betty's Pluck It Cake made with cinnamon and nuts which was served before gifts were opened under the tree. Christmas dinner was formal with ham, curried fruit, and other family recipes eaten around that kitchen table.

Smoking killed my mother-in-law in the end. Bladder cancer, the direct result of years of cigarettes, killed her. An ileostomy permitted one good year of life in which she continued to function as church secretary before the cancer metastasized. I can still see her, cigarette in hand in the hospital, telling my husband to quit smoking.

Twenty-five radiation treatments followed her surgery. Betty lived long enough to see her oldest grandson graduate from high school and gain admission to the honors college at the University of South Carolina in Columbia, where her father served as Board Chairman for thirty-four years.

The day of her death the family physician made a house call to tell us the end was near. Around 7:00 p.m. that night, Betty slipped into a coma as she lay in the same tester bed in which she conceived her children with her husband and children all present. My husband and I wrapped around each other on a single cot at the foot of the bed where family members kept vigil through her final illness. We listened as Betty's breathing slowed and finally stopped.

I knew my mother-in-law for only a very short time – about nine years. During those years, I learned from her what it means to be a virtuous woman, a gem beyond price.

"Who can find a virtuous woman? For her price is far above rubies."(Proverbs 31:10.)

Today when I wear the gold and ruby ring she often wore, my thoughts turn toward her. It is my favorite piece of jewelry.

Hating Miss Hannah
by Dianne Johnson

1 "I could just strangle you!" That's what people say sometimes during an argument and the people involved (or whoever hears) know that it's not going to happen. No one's going to strangle anyone. But she meant it when she said deliberately and slowly and calmly—"I will kill you. I *will* kill you. I will *kill* you."

And he was there. My husband was right there. He was there and didn't say a thing when his mother said matter-of-factly that she would kill me. Didn't say: "This is my wife." Didn't say: "In a Christian household, we don't behave this way." Didn't say: "Mama!" Didn't say: "Mama the baby's watching." Just stood there in the living room like he wasn't there at all.

Sky was almost two. Potty-trained already. She stood there and peed. Right on that off-white carpet.

2. "When did your feelings change about me, Miss Hannah?" I couldn't pinpoint it myself. Couldn't remember when I'd stopped braiding her hair, something one doesn't do for a person who she has bad feelings about. And you don't let just anybody in your hair. Remember in Gloria Naylor's book *Mama Day*, when CoCo

lets the wrong person in her hair? She gets poisoned, and that's it for CoCo. Miss Hannah let me in her hair. She sat and chatted with me at my nephew's baseball games. We made weekly trips to KFC to eat that liver.

"When did it change, Miss Hannah?"

"It changed when you were in the hospital when Sky was born," she said.

"What are you talking about?!"

"I was supposed to be first to know she was born. But your nephew—he's a child. The child knew first. He called up to me, 'Miss Hannah, it's a girl! Her name is Sky!' But I'm the grandmother. I'm supposed to be first to know. And you didn't.... You didn't.... You never talked to me about the things women talk about together."

"That's not true Miss Hannah. How else would I know that when you gave birth you had so much milk, such over-flowing milk, you fed other mothers' children. So much milk."

3.   My husband said to me: "You wouldn't let her feed Sky."

"How could I? I breastfed for eight months. What did you want me to do?"

Later I said to him, "What did you want me to do when she screamed at me that 'Sky has no business being a... what do you call it? Vegetarian?! What's a vegetarian? A child needs meat.'

I told her the doctor says Sky is healthy. He says her skin is honey brown, sun-kissed brown, with a blush that says 'healthy.' She's the picture of health, the doctor says."

But my husband said nothing. No. I'm wrong. He did say something. He said to me: "You are saying something bad about my mother."

4. I hate Miss Hannah because she made me not myself. I walked by her door in the morning. And when I heard Katie Couric on the television, I thought, Shit! She's still alive. I don't want to be a person who thinks like this.

But my husband, Miss Hannah's husband— I mean son—my husband said I wasn't a nice person at all. As soon as Miss Hannah started saying bad things about me, my husband saw everything bad in me, interpreted everything I said or did in the most wicked way he could.

"You're not shy. Just arrogant," he told me. "Your friends and family stick by you only because, well, they're stuck. And I'm stuck!" he yelled. "I have to put up with you," he yelled.

No you don't, I yelled inside myself. No you don't.

5. Miss Hannah yelled at me that I lived with her son before we were married. But I'm confused. Miss Hannah had a husband. And a daughter, for whom she never got piano lessons. That would've been too easy. Just ask any lady at the church. Finding a free piano teacher is easy. Miss Hannah never found her daughter a teacher.

And she divorced her husband for twenty-five dollars. I heard her tell her friend on the telephone, laughing. "That's all it cost me for my divorce," she cackles. But she didn't get the second husband she wanted. My husband's father.

The way I've pieced it together, this is how the story goes: She got pregnant on purpose. He left her before the baby was born. They didn't live far from each other. The boy grew up knowing his father. Could ride his bicycle to visit.

In time, the father got married to someone else and had a daughter seventeen years younger than the son. Years later, the father and his family and Miss Hannah ended up living in the same building in Brooklyn. More time passed. The son, in his fifties, was engaged to me. The father's wife died, and he proposed to Miss Hannah. They didn't marry but were great companions until his death.

6.   My husband once was the lover of a famous singer. When I first went to Miss Hannah's apartment, a photograph of that singer whose name everybody knows was placed so that it was the first thing I saw.

7.   And then there was the move, so I asked him, "Was it your decision or hers for Miss Hannah to move away from her home?" This is what he heard: "I don't want your mother to live with us."

This is what he said: "She lives in a little apartment. It's not a home."

But he didn't see. He didn't see her church family and her apartment building family. He didn't hear the children sing "Good morning Miss Hannah." He didn't feel the glowing of her face when she was in her little space that she called "home," not "my apartment."

Almost crying, she managed to accuse me, somehow, for what he did. "He threw away all of my things. And brought me here. My treasures…." She should have told him.

8.   I can be moody and rude, sometimes. But I am not cruel. I am kind, people say, and pretty. Nicer and prettier than the genius, drug-addict singer. But she can be excused anything, my husband declared, because she is an artist.

9.   I am good. And twenty-seven years younger than my husband. I am smart. When I met him, I had my Ph.D. already. He fell in love with me when he read my dissertation.

But Miss Hannah announced that I'm nothing more than an educated fool.

"If *my* mama said it, there must be something to it," he says, looking straight into my eyes.

10. Many times when I walked into the house, I heard Miss Hannah slandering me in the most casual yet vicious way as she spoke on the phone to her friend. She got the biggest laugh (the biggest I'd heard out of her) from the idea that I thought I could be a writer of books, she said.

11. I came home from my mama's house and went up to Miss Hannah's room to see how her day had been. Something was funny about her face.

"He had to… he had to drag me up off the floor. Into bed. Off the floor," she slurred.

So I called down to him and said, "I think she's had a stroke."

I drove them to the hospital. I am an educated fool who has plenty common sense.

12. I still can't figure out why I never called 911 when my tube ruptured. The baby was in the wrong place. We called my sister, and then we called a cab when we feared she might take too long. When the doctor touched my abdomen, lightly—like a butterfly—my screams filled the air.

"Operating room! Now!"

"Three minutes," the doctor told me later. "Three minutes later and you would've been dead."

But, I reminded myself, Sky was going to get here one way or another.

13. "Well she can't live forever," he tells his buddy. "Mama can't live forever."

Do you pray for long life, Miss Hannah, when you go to church every Wednesday and Sunday? I wonder.

14. It was none of her business. It was private. It was between us. The *akuaba* doll. The Akan doll from Ghana that would help us get pregnant again. And he showed it to her.

15. That started the whole thing. I don't know what she saw exactly. But that started the whole thing. I hear her tell her daughter, who never learned to play piano, that Sky hit me. Ten-month-old Sky hit me. And that I don't know how to discipline a child. And he can't see what's going on in front of his own eyes.

She goes on. "If Sky behaves that way with me, I'll have to hit her and tell them why," she said.

My husband says that his mother was incapable of putting her hands on a child. "She never put her hands on me!" he declared.

16. "You won't let her be a grandmother," he accused me.

The elder women I grew up around would've said: "Girl, let me watch this baby while you take yourself a bath. Girl, you *better* let me help."

But I paid a college girl to feed the baby and wash the baby and put the baby to bed, even while the daddy and the grandmother were in the house.

17. My great grandmother died of sin-sickness. Four husbands. Three too many for her day. Sin-sickness. So they laid her out on the cooling board. And the ceremonies of death began. White wreath on the door. Mirrors covered. Clock covered. Covered dishes of food. Folks talking about my great grandmama, keeping her alive a little longer in their hearts. But she's not passed over yet, not yet. She told our mother/father God that if she was given her life back, she would bring other lives into the world. And she

came back! Praise the lord! People still speak her name, all around the county. If she was there, no matter how difficult the delivery, if she was there, "Everything gonna be all right. Praise God!"

18. "I will kill you."

19. My husband's childhood friend told me that Miss Hannah used to beat my husband close to death. Not a turn of speech. Not an idiom. But a real-life condition, close to death. She stopped only when she saw that he had a special gift. A special talent. Magic in his hands.

20. "I *will* kill you."

21. We were supposed to go to Denver the next day. I have two friends there who had never met Sky.

"You're supposed to be going to see me get the award," he growled. "Not to show off Sky."

I slept that night with Sky, the door locked from the inside. We were out of the house by six. I made plans to move. He flew to Denver and called me that night to tell me the telephone number in his hotel room.

22. My sister friends asked, implored really: "Miss Hannah, did you really say those things to her?!"

Miss Hannah replied, growled really: "Yeah, I said I was gonna kill her!

It took my three sister friends, in their thirties, to pull an eighty-something year-old woman off of me.

"This has nothing to do with you," Miss Hannah told my niece. "I love you."

"You love her enough," I said, "to kill her aunt."

23. I hate Miss Hannah because she has made me homeless.

24. "I thought I married a nice southern girl who knows how to treat her elders," my husband said.

"Talk to your elders," I advised him. I had talked to his elders, to Miss Hannah's brother who swore she had always been mean.

"This is not the insecurity of getting old," he assured me. But I do not tell my husband this.

"Talk to your elders."

"I *am* an elder." End of conversation.

25. My grandmother, the midwife's daughter, told me I should have pushed Miss Hannah down the stairs.

My dear friends from Nigeria told me: "At home, we would call her a witch."

26. This is the story of Miss Hannah and her grandson. He was tall and talented. "A good catch," she thought. Then his girlfriend, who was young, had a disabling stroke. He took her in. I would be so proud, each and every family member thought, to have a grandson like him. But Miss Hannah's only remark was: "But he hasn't married her yet. Just waiting for the right one to come along. Hasn't married her yet."

27. My friend calls me "Turtle." What does that mean? Does it mean that I am self-possessed? That I am at home within myself? Or that I hide from whatever's going on? Does it mean that I am patient and steady or just not assertive enough? Am I tough on the outside, but of no substance inside? I try to be a good turtle.

Did you have a nickname Miss Hannah?

28. When my husband was out of town, Miss Hannah told me over and over again, "Before he met you, he told me he bought this house for me."

29. When my husband was out of town, Miss Hannah called her friend, who was my husband's friend, who has known me since before I was married. Miss Hannah calls this friend and says, gagging and gasping for breath: "His wife is killing me. My heart's going. She's killing me."

30. This is my mother's day story: "Good morning, Honey. Want to go to brunch with me?"

"No, Mama wants to go to the movies." End of conversation.

I had brunch with my sister and niece, after dropping my husband and Miss Hannah off on their date.

31. When both my husband and I were out of town, my too nice sister took Miss Hannah to the grocery store, to the pharmacy, wherever she needed to go. My too-nice sister is a single mother of a son who goes to Yale. She was working on her Ph.D. She always had time for Miss Hannah.

My husband had not raised any of his three sons. My husband took my too-nice sister to small claims court for a few hundred dollars he lent her years ago. Their memories of repayment clashed. Who can find a canceled check from that long ago?

"I have to take her to court," he says, "to teach her about responsibility."

My too-nice sister was still nice to Miss Hannah.

32. This is another day's story: "The role of the lover is the same as the role of the artist. If I love you, I have to make you conscious of the things you don't see."

I was sick to death of hearing that. At the end of every interview and presentation. But that time he was speaking to me.

He continued: "I have to make you conscious, so you won't raise our daughter to be the same kind of person you are. But actually, I shouldn't worry," he said, "she's already different from you. She's not going to use her beauty to get over."

In my pettiness I think, thank goodness she didn't inherit Miss Hannah's hook nose.

33. My husband didn't see. He could no longer see the difference between fact and fiction. I heard him on the phone, telling his buddy that he had to sign the papers, so I could buy a new car. He asked me the next day if he signed papers when we were at the dealership.

"No," I reply.

"Then why was I there," he asked.

"It's a family car. I wanted you to be a part of getting it."

"What family are you talking about?!" He barks.

"You, me, Sky, and your mother."

"My mother! I can count the number of times she's been in that car," he said.

But I said, "It still gets all the groceries, takes us to the doctor, to the movies, all that good stuff."

He shook his head. "I don't know what family you're talking about."

34. At my family reunion, the thirty-fifth, I think, Miss Hannah stood to introduce herself at the huge, formal Thanksgiving dinner, at least one hundred fifty people. But she spoke quietly. A true Oscar performance. I stood up, wanting to make sure everyone knew she was my mother-in-law, not just another distant aunt. But she was livid. I embarrassed her, she said, treated her like a child I had to get up behind. My heart sank.

35. Before I could finish telling her why I am gone, this friend, who was my husband's friend, too, says: "The woman is evil."

Evil is not a word this friend utters lightly. She was my husband's friend.

"I knew you were in trouble the first time I walked in that house," said another, who knew.

36. I'm gone. Where our wedding picture once stood is a picture of my husband and Miss Hannah, taken by me at Thanksgiving.

37. I hate Miss Hannah because she reminds me of Pablo Neruda's words: "Love is so short. Forgetting is so long."

38. I am gone. I am gone so that Sky won't be a good southern girl. So that Sky can adore her Daddy. So that Sky won't know Miss Hannah, really. I am gone because I am tired of hating Miss Hannah.

I am gone to find the home and the god in my turtle heart.

A Southern Union

by Noa Daniels

I t is said that men marry their mothers. I would have loved to have seen the looks on our faces if someone had walked into a room and said that in front of my mother-in-law and me.

My mother-in-law was a "lady," South Carolina born and bred, with straight posture and eyes that took in every detail. You were stupid if you presumed to know what went on behind that sweet smile. She was Southern grace and hospitality, adept in the planning, hosting, and staging of perfect tables with the ultimate achievement of appropriately seating and entertaining her guests.

An accomplished cook in age old recipes of Southern traditions, her food was divine and her recipes detailed down to the brand names of the ingredients and the particular sizes of the bowls or containers in which they were presented or stored. The number of eggs added to create a particular dish often determined the excellence of a dish. I paid attention when she taught me how to prepare a recipe, more from fear than admiration at the time.

Her knowledge extended from flowers and gardening to fashion and protocols. She was a beauty queen, a college graduate, a teacher, and a wife. She was a mother who made sure her children knew their social graces and perfectly demonstrated their Southern manners. She did the right things. She knew the right people.

She was brought up in staunch tradition, like the starched perfection of an impeccably ironed dress, delivered in no-nonsense fashion from the ironing board of the maid who deftly pressed it. Her stories, like her friends and relatives, made connections to people and places like lines dropping down in genealogy charts from generation to generation.

I viewed her as one from a foreign country.

I was a rural Virginia, tomboy implant, grafted into the state of South Carolina in 1962 in the month of April when alien plants such as wisteria and Spanish moss dripped off the trees, and the azaleas exploded into color. Everywhere, flowers of every shape, size, and color crowded the landscape while clouds of pollen consumed the air and transformed familiar objects into curious forms outlined in powdery yellow.

My brothers and sister, intrigued with their new surroundings, joyfully introduced my family to the flavors of soft, salty, slimy oddities known as boiled peanuts and okra. I soberly pondered them all.

In those days, my mother-in-law stood like a tall, impenetrable tower. But that was before the crack in the wall, before the breach of infidelity which would ultimately destroy the perfect picture and the rose-colored glass upon which she, and other Southern females of her generation, so carefully built their foundations.

Many of these proud stately towers filled small Southern towns—towers of social graces and knowing smiles, crafted in wealth or the perception of it. Towers made of notions of things concocted by the mind, a community of females bound in allegiance to social conventions which were and are still proudly celebrated, honored, and passed down, unspoken social norms and rules of behavior on which all "acceptable" Southern society operates. They stood on appearances, fabrications of life as it should be. Fabrications that often secretly and silently destroyed their lives and families, and are perpetuated still, but perhaps not as much as in those days.

The greatest standard of Southern life, venerated and at the heart of the art of Southern living, is family—the strongest bond, the heart of the home, the heart of life, the one true standard that when violated, could bring a tower crashing down. Ironic that these norms, so revered as to be imposed on and ingrained in families, would virtually define an upstanding family, yet would quite often be the very wedge between its family members which could force those who should be "held so dearly," to instead be held "at arm's length."

In her day, "I love you" was an expression was rarely heard, but rather, understood. And I, who had been wrapped in my mother's arms could not understand her. But when the tower fell, I beheld the creation of another kind of Southern Union.

For underneath it all, there is a soul in a Southern woman which carries itself in quiet strength. Perhaps it is genetic, passed down from a people whose history is well acquainted with adversity and sorrow. And while my mother-in-law mourned for lost love and a way of life that was disappearing, I witnessed a life destroyed, razed to its very foundation.

At sixteen, I fell in love with her son. As she watched me grow through the years, it became evident that his feelings and mine were mutual. I'm not sure she approved, though she never spoke the words, but I imagined I could feel her disapproval. For I, a foreign object, had come in and stormed the tower.

After years of a tumultuous relationship, her son and I married. And after our union, she and I circled each other: she, the quietly sweet, Southern passive-aggressive, and I, the revolutionary confrontationist. But over time, my mother-in-law and I began to understand our individual boundaries. We came to mutually recognize and respect the customary "three-days of company" enjoyment limit.

And through the years, though I never shared the arms that I sometimes longed to be held in, I shared her life through the exchange of thoughts, stories, tears, and fears not even expressed to her own children. And when she discovered the crack in her foundation and the tower fell, I fought beside her. I fought for her, trying to hold her up with my own strength.

When it was over and I viewed the rubble, I thought her life destroyed. But I had underestimated my mother-in-law and her love of family. Out of that debris emerged a woman, a wounded, solitary figure, who slowly, painstakingly began to rebuild her life.

I have learned that people cannot be measured by appearances, for what is the difference in the strength of those who charge headlong, swords drawn, into the clash of battle and the strength of those who tend the wounded and dead, or those who must face a life in which they have lost everything? Perhaps it is all just perception.

My mother-in-law poured out her life for her family. When my children or I were sick, or I had no one to help me, she was always there. She appeared without being asked and did what had to be done. She cooked meals, tended fevers, or sat quietly beside the sick while they slept. She willing did whatever she had to do to maintain her family and the relationships with her children. She was a great friend to her friends, a treasure trove of information, a constant at family gatherings or funerals.

As one will find true of many Southerners, she was unique and a delight. She taught us all the values of her life by living those principles before us. Her life was a testament of love.

While my mother-in-law and I still did not always see eye to eye on things, we shared much and agreed on much. She taught me about cooking and gardening and arranging flowers. She encouraged me in a way few others have ever done to pursue my talents.

In my mind's eye, a monument now stands upon the ruins of a tower. It represents a lifetime and a life given to others. It testifies to the grace and charm of a particular, strong, Southern woman—my mother-in-law.

When I think of her now (and I often do), two words stand out: reverence and gratitude—reverence for her quiet strength and gratitude for her generosity, inspiration, and impact on my own family and life.

Thank you, dear "Mimi." I am so proud of you and of this family we've formed together.

Mart 'Ami

by Lillian McCarter Batarseh

Note: Mart 'Ami (literally, wife of uncle) means Mother-in-law in Arabic. This is what I called my amazing Palestinian mother-in-law.

You were so beautiful walking past the outdoor café where your future husband, having drinks on a Mediterranean holiday, emphatically declared to his companion at the table, "That's the girl I'm going to marry!"

➤ 'Twas the seaside resort of Jaffa, Palestine, in the early 1930s. Salt in the air, bright sun overhead. A young man of just the right age to be searching for Miss Perfect. What's not to like about silky olive skin, magnetic brown eyes, a warm smile, and ample curves? So the two men surreptitiously followed to see where she lived. Thus it was, that after investigation by Hanna's (i.e., John's) clan from Bethlehem of the character and social standing of the aforementioned attractive young lady, an entourage led by Hanna's father made an appointment with Mahfouz Amireh in Jaffa to arrange for the hand of his lovely daughter. And the rest, as they say, is history.

Despite the cultural strictures on women in the thirties, you were the original "I-am-woman-hear-me-roar" girl, standing—literally—on a soapbox to denounce the British, whom you feared would give away your country.

> It was not that she didn't like the British. After all, her husband worked as a contractor providing services (food, laundry, and the like) for the British army camps implementing their League of Nations mandate in Palestine. He was an interpreter with the rank of sergeant in the Scottish Black Watch regiment in Gaza. He even wore a kilt! Then, too, her family socialized with the British officers, often inviting them into their home for drinks and dinner. The problem was a political one: the British had made two incompatible promises— one to the Arabs (including the Palestinians) of independence for significantly aiding the British during World War I, and the other promise to European Zionists wishing to establish a homeland for the Jews in Palestine. Neither side thought that the British were doing enough for their cause. Complications abounded, even within each side. Around 1937, Hanna's father, a much respected freelance advocate who often appeared in court on his clients' behalf, was killed on his way home in Bethlehem. Previously, the family home had been shot up by factions who did not appreciate his refusal to help pay for their violent activities against the British, and there was speculation, though never proven, that these same people were responsible for the assassination. Whatever their methods of protest, peaceful or violent, the Palestinians

were angry with the British for allowing the immigration of hundreds of thousands of non-native Jews, who were establishing enclaves in the land and secretly arming themselves for future battle.

When the catastrophe came and all was lost—even the baby pictures—the family immigrated to a foreign land, and you made for your five little refugees a refuge there.

➤ In 1948, the state of Israel was established. What was Independence Day for the Zionists was for the Palestinian Arabs the Nakba—the Catastrophe. Over 700,000 of these native inhabitants of the land were either driven from their homes or left (briefly they thought "until things blew over") to find safe haven. Hanna, having moved by this time to Jerusalem in order to run the family's Holy Land souvenir shop there, wanted to get his family out of danger. His longtime friends and Jewish neighbors had a standing arrangement of Friday night dinner at alternating homes with Hanna and Mart 'Ami. The friends offered shelter and relative safety at their apartment, but Mart 'Ami and her husband refused in order not to put the Jewish family in jeopardy and also to have all the extended Batarseh family together to weather the storm. It turned out to be a veritable hurricane. Homes and farms and orchards and businesses were taken over. Sometimes whole villages—such as Deir Yassein—were wiped out. Books and libraries were expropriated. The family, along with many others, was never able to return to their homes and belongings. Eventually, since the tourist industry was wiped out during the fighting and work was impossible to find, they moved to Egypt and carved out a new life. For a long time, years in fact, they lived quite modestly. But with much hard work, Hanna became owner of a prosperous steel making factory near Cairo. Though safe, Mart 'Ami had to raise her children without the traditional family support that would have been her due back home. Other family members fared less well. Their fate is captured in the following poem, written in response to our single photograph of the gentle maternal grandfather wearing a fez. ("*Jiddi*" means "Grandfather".)

O Blue-Eyed *Jiddi*

You with the deft hands of the silversmith

You whose children ran in early morn

down to the sea

to buy those tiny sardines

straight from the boat

for Grandmother to prepare

with *tahini* sauce in a large tray

to be sent to the communal oven

and baked for a tantalizing breakfast

You who graciously held *diwan*

in the huge salon

of your four-thousand-square-foot mansion

You who blessedly did not live to see

your wife and children leave it behind

during the *Naqba*,

never to return,

or your son in the railroad center of Lydda

who had to trudge with his family
on foot to Ramallah
and watch helplessly as your
daughter's-in-law gold jewelry was removed
from its hiding place in her bra
by armed usurpers
who would not heed her plea
to at least leave her wedding ring,
How can you stay so calm under your red fez?

Though you'd been away for decades you were so special that at your passing, a memorial service was held in Bethlehem. Everyone came from miles around.

> After one year of marriage and the completion of my husband's PhD at the University of South Carolina, we moved, as planned, to the Middle East, intending to stay forever. But forever lasted only eighteen months (the move, that is; the marriage is still intact). So my time with my mother-in-law was short, but oh so sweet. I witnessed her generosity from the time of my engagement during my senior year at Winthrop College when she and others in both the Cairo and Bethlehem contingents of the family celebrated the event by sending me an amethyst ring the size of New Jersey.

Soon after our arrival in Bethlehem, my in-laws flew in from Cairo to visit. Mart 'Ami came bearing gifts: purses and reams of lovely Egyptian cotton material to be made into frocks, as was the custom there in the '60s.

But it was her generosity of spirit that made her so special to me. It made no difference to her that I was not Arab or Catholic or that I might be a tad too tall and more than a tad too skinny. If her eldest son loved me, she would love me too. And she did, in a myriad of ways, from calling my name with a lovely lilt to later supporting me as a young mother an ocean away from my own mother and with only Dr. Spock as a guide.

She prepared fantastic meals for us when we visited Cairo and planned fun trips such as having the family chauffeur drive us out to the edge of the city to have my picture taken sitting on a camel and to snake our way with other tourists into the inner recesses of the pyramids. She introduced me to the delicacies at Cairo's world famous *Groppi's* ice cream and pastries shop, took us to meet her friends for a dinner of gigantic shrimp at a Swiss chalet overlooking the pyramids, and even took us on a get-away with her and 'Ami for a few days of R&R on the magnificent beaches of Alexandria. This, of course, was during the harvest time of her life.

The folks back in Bethlehem knew Mart 'Ami through thick and thin and remembered her vivacious personality and courageous attitude throughout her life. They recalled how she had supported her husband in his political life and efforts to protect and better the community. They knew of her rare knack for talking chefs at favorite restaurants out of their prize recipes and then serving these dishes to her friends in her home. They remembered her struggles to feed her family during World War II rationing, when regular foodstuffs were hard or impossible to find.

There, too, many knew her for her boldness in a male dominated society. Although her husband worked hard and was a good provider for the family's needs, there were times when he spent too much time hanging out with male buddies in Jerusalem's bars. When this happened, Mart 'Ami would sally forth into the bar, where no other woman dared to go, and drag him home by the earlobe, causing his friends to jokingly call her the MP. Though "just a housewife," Mart 'Ami was cosmopolitan, well-educated, and able to hold her own with people of all stripes and stations.

Some of this must have rubbed off onto her offspring, for among the five, there would be two physicians (an ob/gyn and an ear, nose, and throat specialist), a psychologist/professor, a teacher, and an engineer. Moreover, one married a Palestinian, another an American, the third a Lebanese living in Egypt (whose family wound up in Brazil), and the youngest a Spanish speaking woman from Colombia, South America! Bethlehem's most indelible memory of Mart 'Ami, however, was her dedication to the people of Palestine when they poured into town by the thousands, most with only what they could carry, during the Nakba crisis, filling schools and churches and mosques. She, Helaneh Amireh Batarseh, not only continued to care for her household as a refugee herself, but poured out her heart and energies in collecting, organizing, and distributing donated food, blankets, and clothing to those in need—Moslems and Christians alike.

*****

And besides all this that you accomplished, when I whined one day that I couldn't think of anyone to write about, your son (with not an iota of modesty) urged, "Why don't you write about my mother? After all, she produced for you a great husband!"

Flip Flops
by Krista Bowes

"AGH!" She bolts upright. "You scared the *shit* out of me!"

It's so easy to scare the shit out of my mother-in-law—too easy: a pump of the car brakes, a sneeze, a cabinet closed too hard, anytime her back is turned towards the door and I pop my head inside to ask a quick question. Always the same, "AGH! Oh my god, you scared the shit out of me!"

Other people startle; Patti jumps and grabs at herself. Over the past twelve years, I've learned to make noise before turning a corner, or entering a room, or walking down a hallway. I've tried clearing my throat first; sometimes that works. Maybe that's why my father-in-law constantly whistles. That way she always knows where he is, like a kitten with a bell on his collar.

At this point in her reading this, she has most likely guffawed, thrown her head back, stomped her foot, and rocked herself backwards in her rocking chair. (She is always in her rocker because she likes to keep moving.) Her whole face has filled with laughter which has undoubtedly spilled over her eyes and down her cheeks, and she has said aloud, "Ooooh me, that was good."

Unlike myself, Patti lives out loud. If a line is crossed, you'll know it. If clothing is too big or too small, or if she thinks you're crazy, she'll tell you.

She wears bright colored t-shirts with matching flip-flops, so many flip-flops. I own three pairs of flip-flops: brown, black, and navy. She doesn't like being snubbed in the fabric store and tells the manger what she thinks. She sends back her overcooked pancakes, while I simply add more syrup. She doesn't care for sausage and likes her bacon extra crispy. I love it all. She leaps when ice is spilled in her lap. I don't move because, well, the worst is over, right? Then I'll stand up, dumping ice to the floor, and we both bend down to pick up the ice.

She's impulsive, the over-doer. She chips my plates in the sink while washing them. She scratches my hardwood floors when she vacuums under the furniture, and I will gladly take all that because she takes all of me.

She doesn't let me apologize for traits I consider flaws in my personality. I over-think to the point of sadness. I analyze and stall until the perfectionist in me wins, paralyzing. She says that's what makes me Krista, and she wouldn't have me any other way because she knows that under all that mental mess is a heart that means well.

She sees who I could be if I believed in myself as she believes in me, if I had even one ounce of the confidence she has always had in me.

But I fail to generate it in myself. So, I'll keep her, for better or worse, as she has kept me.

At this point in her reading of this, she is most likely still rocking in her chair and wiping her cheeks. Her eyes brim again with tears, but not from laughter this time—from her swelling heart—because she loves her daughter from another mother.

As for me: I just wish I wore a size 8 ½. I do envy her collection of flip-flops.

Sex and My Mother-in-Law: A Tale of Wifely Duties

by Roxie Ann Hunter

Right after we graduated college, my former husband and I lived with his parents for a while. His folks were in their mid-fifties and appeared almost oppressively straight-laced. So I was understandably shocked when they invited us to go with them to the...uh, local non-PG movie house one night.

Now don't get me wrong. I was by no means a prude and had lived through the 60s and early 70s with colorful stories to tell, but I had never seen a dirty movie—and I certainly never expected to see one with my in-laws who were right out of a Grant Wood painting. Jim and I were amazed by the invitation—and a bit weirded out.

But we agreed to go. And anyway, they were treating.

It turns out my mother-in-law hated pornography of any kind, but she felt it was her wifely duty to go with her husband, so he wasn't out there on his own doing God-knows-what. (Not that he ever was.) So after dinner, we piled into the family station wagon,

The Fascist

by Laura P. Valtorta

My relationship with my mother-in-law is an uncomfortable mess of jealousy, hatred, admiration, exasperation, and cultural gap. Her first language is Italian, mine, English. I couldn't talk with her or understand her endless monologues, until I learned Italian.

We are both the oldest of three sisters. She is a teacher; I am a lawyer. She lives in Italy; I live in the United States. Since 1981, we have been in a tug of war—we love the same man—Marco, my husband, who is an only child.

When Marco and I had our first child on September 10, 1984, we named her "Clara Giulia Valtorta"—"Clara" after my great-grandmother and "Giulia" [pronounced "Julia"] after my mother-in-law, Maria Giulia.

This turned out to be an excellent choice for a middle name because Clara's birth improved my relationship with my mother-in-law ninety-five percent. The jealousy between us almost vanished. We gained some rapport.

I even nearly forgave her for stealing away several fine vacations with my husband, Marco, which should have been romantic adventures, but instead, turned into fights and gross illustrations of the fact that my husband was one gigantic baby.

The memories still cut me like knives. Soon after we were married, Marco spoke at an Artificial Intelligence conference in Karlsruhe, Germany. Karlsruhe was a beautiful city, and we should have had fun, even though Marco proposed we stay in student quarters to save money.

Then came the horrible news.

Marco excitedly announced to me, "My parents will meet us there. They will pay for an expensive hotel! They will be staying with us in the same hotel."

Gone were all chances of a romantic vacation together, alone, without children, in a foreign city I had never seen before. We never had that chance again because our daughter was born eighteen months after we married.

I remember Karlsruhe with anger. We ate breakfast, lunch, and dinner with old people. We traveled to see the sights with old people—my in-laws, who paid for everything.

My father-in-law, Alberto, played just as much a role as my mother-in-law in stealing that experience away from me, but somehow I blamed Maria Giulia more. She was the other woman in my husband's life. Rich and all-powerful. A teacher with forty years of experience. How can you tell a man to avoid seeing his own mother? To stop worshiping her?

The entire country of Italy has an obsession with motherhood. According to a poll in an Italian magazine, the favorite modern song of Italians is "Mamma." All three m's in that word are pronounced with much smacking of lips—"Mamma!"

There is even a special word describing this obsession: "*mammismo.*" The boys who cannot grow away from their mothers are called "*mammoni.*"

Children in Italy typically do not leave home until they finish university, and sometimes, not until after marriage. They often bring their spouses to live with their parents. Living space in Italy is scarce and tight, and the bond between mother and son even tighter.

Given all of this, Marco's parents must be given tremendous credit for allowing their only, pampered, nerd son to travel to America on a Fulbright scholarship to study computer science at Duke University. They encouraged him to go. And when he announced that he and I were dating, that we would get married, they presented little or no opposition. All this, despite the fact they didn't really like me. Many people around the world and in the United States, forbid their children to marry foreigners. But Marco's parents let his happen. They had great respect for Americans, and they never held my American citizenship and upbringing against me.

Maria Guilia did, however, act jealous. She refused to talk to me. She cried and held Marco's hands in hers whenever we were about to leave and return to the States. She displayed a lot of antipathy toward me, which did not abate until Clara was born. A couple of times, Marco's father told her to quit, but this is something you cannot tell a woman: quit being jealous. Women, who are often powerless, feel envy and jealousy, deeply.

My mother-in-law is more intelligent than attractive. Her family name is "Gnocchi," just like the food, the potato pasta. The name is appropriate because that is what she looks like—a potato dumpling. She is short, pale, fat, and nearly bald. Her teeth are cylinders of decay; she has loose, fat lips.

Alberto, who died in 1998, must have felt tremendous love for his wife. He once told me that he had married her because she was the smartest woman he could find. I thought this was the most flattering comment I had ever heard from a man to a woman. They married when they were in their early thirties, just after World War II. Their first child died in infancy.

Alberto had served in the military in the Russian campaign. He was a good-looking ladies' man, known as a *"farfallone"* (big butterfly). Once when Marco and I were living in Belgium and had been married for about four years, I asked Alberto and Maria Giulia to describe their old conquests, the people they dated before marriage. Marco had never questioned them about this. They smiled and went down the list. When Alberto got to a certain red-haired woman who seemed important, I asked where she was now. "I think she's married," he mused, "with three children."

"Three **daughters**," Giulia interjected as though daughters were less valuable than sons (strange coming from the oldest of three daughters.) I took this as an insult to me, the mother of one daughter [at the time], but I said nothing.

As the oldest daughter in her family, Maria Giulia suffered the same fate as I. Although she was the smartest child, her family sent her to the same school as the other two daughters and offered her one option—to be a teacher.

Alberto, on the other hand, had gone to university in place of, and instead of, his numerous brothers and sisters who left school to work after *liceo* [high school]. He was the smartest, and his family recognized this.

Maria Giulia told me that once upon a time when she was thirteen, she had been very thin. I never saw any evidence of this in photographs or written accounts, and I do not believe her. She said she was the leader of a centurion of kids—one hundred kids who marched for Mussolini. Fascism. *Viva Italia!* Square, patriotic buildings and trains running on time. The same Mussolini who offered a return to the greatness of Rome. I can picture Maria Giulia at the head of her hundred kids, leading them and bossing them around.

Then came World War II, bombs dropping. Marco's mother likes to tell the story of taking her teacher's exam in Milan during an air raid. She is a Milanese, a woman of the city, while Alberto came from the countryside.

For forty years, she taught Italian and history at a high school that required more training (a university diploma) than teaching in a grammar school. Her boss and principal was a Sicilian man, a sin that she forgave him explicitly. "He is from Sicily, but he's a wonderful man; he smokes a pipe."

My Italian relatives were from Sicily, of course. Sicily and Calabria.

When I see the color burnt orange, I think of my mother-in-law. Her living room in Milan is decorated in that color. So is her hair—what there is left of it. For a long time, I loathed that color because it reminded me of her and her antique furniture with its hunting theme. There is no air conditioning in Milan except in the banks and supermarkets, but she never lets us open the windows in that apartment, even in the dead heat of August.

"*C'e corrente!*" she whines. "There's a draft!"

Recently, I bought a burnt orange sweater and liked it.

During the *La Dolce Vita* of the 1960s and '70s, Maria Giulia bought four apartments, which was a smart thing to do. We enjoy those apartments now, especially the one on the Italian Riviera. They are small dwellings, tiny, in fact, but they do have bedrooms, bathrooms, and kitchens. The floors are covered in marble and tile. You can cook pasta in these apartments on funny-smelling gas burners. You can take a shower or even a bath if you're lucky. You can use the bidets. In Italy, living space of any kind is difficult to find. Just as Alberto noted, my mother-in-law is intelligent. He resisted buying the property; she insisted.

My mother-in-law's stories about Marco as a child depict him as good and perfect, a terrific kid who always did well in school. As she tells these stories Marco smiles widely, and a halo appears over his head. Never mind that his cousins do not agree. They say he chased them around waving a stick, and he liked to smash batteries to see the stuff inside.

"This could not possibly be true," huffs Marco's mother. "He was always good. Perfect. A treasure!"

She will admit, however, that as a small kid on vacation in the mountains, Marco broke the hotel's washing machine. He led a band of kids into the laundry room, and they shut off the water while the washing machine was running. The motor burned out. Marco's parents were banished from that resort forever.

She also admits that Marco has a weird ritual involving wristwatches. Marco enjoys buying watches that claim they are "water resistant," or better yet, "waterproof" to a certain number of meters. He buys these watches and then wears them while diving into deep water. The watches always break. He turns them in and gets a refund.

Obtaining the refund seems to afford him gleeful satisfaction. When Marco's mother whispered that seemed "somewhat strange," it was, for me, like winning the lottery.

"Marco *is* strange," I thought. "And his mother agrees."

Usually Maria Giulia knows more about the Valtortas than I do, but there was one instance when I knew a lot more. It happened as Alberto lay dying of cancer in 1998. I wrote her a letter describing things I remembered most about Alberto. He and I enjoyed watching movies together. He was a smart businessman with lots of friends. He was handsome and wore his clothes well.

I also included a story he had told Marco and me about his service in the Italian army during World War II. His troop was ordered into Russia where the winter soon caused many fatalities. Men were freezing to death, and Alberto had frost bite in his feet. His commanding officer wanted to proceed further into Russia, but Alberto had other ideas. He pulled a gun on the officer and said, "We're heading back."

The soldiers turned around and avoided being trapped. Russian families helped them along the way, which was one of the reasons Alberto decided to build appliance plants in Communist countries following the war. He always liked the Russians.

I assumed that Alberto had told his wife this story since he told Marco and me. Pulling the gun on a commanding officer was a dramatic move to make and probably saved a lot of lives. But his military career ended in disgrace, which seemed a minor point.

When Maria Giulia read this letter, she was astonished. It was the first time she had heard the story. Giorgi, Alberto's youngest brother, had not heard it either. He asked Alberto, who confirmed the story before he died.

In 1995, Marco and I had a son, Dante Bruno. When Dante was a newborn, he resembled Alberto, which alarmed me, but gave my in-laws a lot of pleasure. These days, six-year-old Dante looks like my family and me. I feel myself spoiling him. Dante needs a lot of hugs, and so do I.

When I hug Dante or pat his curly hair, I think about Maria Giulia. Relationships between mother and son are special. They are sexual, almost, and innocent at the same time. What if Dante grows up and gets married? What if he chooses a wife who hates me? What if I interfere too much in his life?

Right now, I predict I will make a conscious effort to avoid interference. I will not be the evil mother-in-law. I will stay away from Dante the adult. Avoid visiting him. As an old woman, I will travel to Singapore, tour the Grand Canyon, and perhaps buy an apartment in Pasadena.

Certainly, I will not require Dante to travel across an ocean to be with me five times a year. I will not refuse to walk outside unless he helps. I will not report soccer results to him over the phone every Sunday, or lure him back home with money.

I will not do any of these things in thirty years. Or will I?

Learning Compassion
by Michelle Ross

Not every woman has a relationship with her husband's mother. In Old World China, the daughter-in-law serves her husband's mother at the whim of the mother-in-law. But since modernization, that tradition exists mostly in small rural communities.

Surprisingly, in our society, there seems an expectation that as soon as vows are exchanged, the mother-in-law rises to the status of mother. I do not think I have ever understood that particular expectation, especially since I have had three MILs.

But regardless, these three women gave birth to the men I have loved, and because of that, it has been my responsibility to respect and learn something about each of them.

*****

Every piece of furniture, table cloth, and doily adorned the rooms of Alice Mae's home in blues and the colors of spring flowers. A school teacher, devout member of an Independent Baptist Church, and mother of three children, Alice Mae never raised her voice in anger. I remember the day my first husband Doug told me that he nor his siblings had ever heard their parents argue. Each were born into and raised in what seemed a perfect, genteel home environment. I am convinced my first mother-in-law's sweet voice and contagious giggle kept peace in the house, and it further kept at bay the wolf lurking between crevices, at least for a while.

She and I bonded in ways that only strengthened as this wolf made its presence increasingly visible, even after my first marriage ended. Demanding attention were issues like alcoholism, drug addiction, paternal emotional neglect. Such a brilliant family, but Alice Mae's blues and springtime colors not only kept the wolf of dysfunction at bay, they muted the voices of her children and attempted to block-out the life-producing, necessary freeze of winter.

Still, both the wolf and winter eventually emerged. By choice, the oldest child chose to live in another state, not for opportunity but to distance himself from his father. Everybody in the household knew it. But because his love for his mother ran deep, he moved away to protect her from the anger that ran deep within him, and he didn't trust himself to keep his anger out of the house.

The second child, a theatre and voice major, filled the home with Disney-like song. But on a day well into my relationship with her younger brother, she approached me in tears. In her perception, I was closer to her father than she had ever been.

At that time, her statement confused me. My family was not one of springtime hues, but closer to the heat of summer and chill of autumn. We were a family of raw emotion and hid very little, either positive or negative, from one another.

I believe it was this rawness of emotion that attracted her father to me; it also laid the foundation for developing a relationship with Alice Mae. The more her life fell apart, the more intimate our talks became.

Alice Mae's youngest child, Doug, was my first and defining love. Although he did not create physical distance like his older brother, nor face conflicting emotions like his sister Jan, Doug found solace in drugs, alcohol, and playing (cards, tennis, golf, football, and basketball).

Groomed to be sky blue and springtime colors, he spared his mother from his addictions and pain. I, on the other hand, spared her nothing. After our marriage ended, Alice saw the rawness of my emotions and their unsophisticated manifestation of confusion and pain. Again, that's where she and I connected most deeply.

So often Alice stated with a sigh how the sun rose and set on her husband. But after 40 years of marriage, her sunrise-sunset marriage abruptly ended with alcohol and an affair. With me, Alice Mae could share her unsophisticated emotions, her anger, and pain from the betrayal she felt.

And because she knew I never stopped loving her son and that I never stopped grieving the end of our marriage—even after his early death at 48 years old—she felt comfort that I understood her grief.

Yet even this pain took its toll, but not without signs of mercy. Into her 90s, Alice Mae has her blues and springtime colors again. Dementia brought them back.

Eight years after my divorce from Doug, I met a man with whom I believed I was compatible. We shared the same religion; he was an active member in the community, and we had similar ethnicities. Ron and I also came from the rawness of peasant stock. The connection to his mother Rose (my second mother-in-law) seemed seamless; we baked *kolach* (Eastern European nut bread), ate pickled pig's feet, danced the polka, and hugged and kissed big.

Unfortunately, not only did we share similar ethnicities, we both married men who shared the qualities of Dr. Jekyll and Mr. Hyde. We married darkness. These men admired the leadership of Hitler. Ron once dreamed that he apprenticed under vampires whose prey were the people who loved them most. This rang true to me. I don't believe his or his father's actions came from their own wounded-ness, but rather that as men, they felt entitled.

Few signs of springtime colors bloomed in Rose's home. Instead the hues ranged more like those in sewage.

A plumber, her husband dictated that toilets be flushed no more than once a day and never at night. He dictated everything, and all obeyed.

But just as a wolf lurked in Alice Mae's blues, a spot of color found residence in Rose's bedroom in a framed photo. To say she was beautiful in her younger years is an understatement.

Not without personal dreams, Rose dreamed of becoming an airline stewardess. But her family did not support her dream, and she accepted their lack of support and gave in to them.

From that day forward, her natural beauty waned and her life became one of many resignations. In fact, her loyalty to resignation normalized to such a degree she flinched little at the threatening violent behavior of her husband, nor could she acknowledge the violent nature of Ron, my second husband.

And I remember after the sudden death of her oldest son, business went on as usual.

She expected me to follow her path of resignation, and I almost did. But after fifteen years of life sucked from me and all five of my children, I said, "No more." Thank goodness there was enough life left in us that we could begin to heal.

After divorcing Ron, Rose and I never connected again, until I received a sympathy card for the death of my third husband, John. By then, I was able to accept her extension of sympathy with returned affection.

To be honest, I should never have married anyone. I am just too much of something: independence, willfulness—something.

Nevertheless, I married another eight years after my divorce from Ron. Bottom line, John melted my icy heart. John's father was an artist born and raised in the North, and he married Flo, who was born and raised in the South. John took after his father; they both made beautiful art. Pieces of their art are positioned throughout my home, his mother's, and in the homes of other family members. John's spirit was as beautiful as his art, and his spirit made miracles.

We met before and fell in love after his diagnosis of incurable prostate cancer. When my heart was still in its icy state, and when John was going through chemo-therapy in North Carolina, he'd regularly call to give updates and to chat. I'd wonder why because at that point, I didn't know him well enough to even care about his health. (Sounds cold, doesn't it?)

But after a few months of phones calls, I noticed a change: I cared. After John's return to South Carolina where we both lived, I met his mother Flo over the phone. At one point in our conversation, she cried in relief that I loved her son and that he would not be alone. Then when John and I exchanged wedding vows, I cried, knowing that we would truly be married "until death do us part."

Little did I know a shock to my system awaited me, and it was a shock from which I still am mending. Both John and his mother went into a state of denial over his prognosis. My role quickly changed from being a sympathetic partner and daughter-in-law to one who had to take complete charge.

Flo and I could not hold hands, we could not comfort one another through John's decline. Nor could John and I journey through his illness together as one.

Completely ignoring obvious signs of weight loss and increased physical disabilities, Flo and John instead made decisions based on the belief of full recovery, up to the day he died. The only saving grace was my strong will that took the necessary actions that kept his body comfortable.

And sadly, Flo remained in shock for a number of years, and we rarely communicated. But five years after John's death I received a letter, and Flo and I began to hold hands. My heart broke for her and accepted with love her brokenness.

I will never be able to say that my relationships with my mothers-in-law were traditional or conventional. But I can say that without them, I could not have found the depth of compassion in me. They have challenged me to go places I would never have gone on my own.

Miss Beth

by Dale Barwick

I first met my mother-in-law the day her only son graduated from college. At the time, Tony and I were not romantically involved; nevertheless, I was nervous about meeting her. Tony rarely talked about his family back home, but he had told me that his mama was a nurse. Just that tidbit of information was enough to intimidate me because I was still a lowly nursing student.

Tony had invited his family members and a few close friends to join him for lunch at Shoney's after graduation. As he introduced his mother to his friends, she threw her hand in the air and said, "I'm Beth."

A dozen of us sat at a long table with Tony in the middle. Miss Beth and I ended up on opposite ends. The entire restaurant filled with excited graduates and well-wishers. The noise level made it almost impossible to carry on a conversation with the person next to me, much less someone at the other end of the table. I felt awkward and out of place with so much claiming Tony's attention.

But then over all the commotion, I heard a man coughing at the table next to us. The lady with him leaned toward him and said, "Are you okay?" Then she yelled out, "Somebody help! He's choking!"

I leapt to my feet and my untested nurses' training jumpstarted my adrenaline. The first thing I thought was: God, help me help this man!

Think, think, think! The first rule in helping choking victims is to see if they are really choking.

I put my hand on the man's shoulder. "Are you choking?" I asked. My heart beat wildly, but the voice coming out of my mouth sounded astonishingly calm and confident.

He nodded and continued to cough.

Assess the airway. Determine if the obstruction is partial or complete. As long as the victim can talk or cough, do not perform back blows or abdominal thrusts.

"Okay, I'll be right here to help you. Let's see if you can cough it out on your own. If not, I'll help you get it out."

The restaurant got quiet, and the man continued to cough, but more weakly, and his face turned pale. I was in the spotlight, right where I hated to be, but I kept my focus on the man. Then, I felt a hand on my back. Tony's mother had come to the rescue. I was more than happy to move away and let a real nurse take control.

"You're doing great," she said quietly in my ear.

Uh oh! I'm still on, I thought.

The man's coughing stopped. His face held a look of panic.

Deliver up to five back blows.

"I'm going to hit you really hard on the back," said the calm voice that was mine. "Just lean forward a little." I glanced at Ms. Beth, and she nodded her encouragement.

I placed my left hand on the man's chest and hit him between the shoulder blades with the heel of my right hand. I drew back to hit him again, but stopped halfway because a hunk of slimy steak landed on the table. The Man took in big gulps of air and leaned back in his chair as the color returned to his face.

"Hoo-wee," he said weakly, and I laughed with relief.

Ms. Beth said to him, "Drink some of your tea, and let's see how you do."

With the excitement over, the other diners returned to their meals and conversations. When it was obvious that he would be all right, the man and his wife thanked us, and we headed back to our table. Miss Beth patted me on the back and said, "Ya did good, kiddo."

Fast-forward six years, two nursing degrees, and a failed marriage to a man who wasn't Tony. The next time I saw Miss Beth, Tony took me to her house for a visit.

The small Southern town they lived in was abuzz with gossip about the divorcee Tony was dating—me. The people of his church didn't approve. It stung, and I felt quietly miserable about it for both our sakes.

We sat on Miss Beth's patio and talked. In her way that I would come to love, she went straight to the point. "You know people are talking about you."

"Yes, ma'am. I know."

"They're saying you're divorced."

"Yes ma'am."

"I tell 'em, 'Yeah, she's been married before.'"

Where are we going with this?

She said, "They ask me if you have any children. And I say, 'Yeah, she does.'"

My back stiffened, and I slid to the edge of my chair. "I don't have…"

She held up her hand. "Let me finish. So, I say, 'Yep, she has one child—with four legs and a tail.' And that shuts 'em right up."

She chuckled. I settled back in my patio chair and grinned.

"Don't let 'em get to ya, honey," she said.

During the ensuing years of my marriage to Tony, the pattern continued. Miss Beth believed in me, encouraged me, stood by me, let me make my own mistakes, and was there when I needed her. She has always had my back. I couldn't ask for anything more.

Lessons in Ms. Thelma's Kitchen
by Kathy China

"How about we go to Gates Street to get some lunch today?" my new partner in the Community-Oriented Policing Program suggested. Since he was older and more experienced than I, his idea sounded fine. I acquiesced, hoping he remembered I was particular about eating a clean diet. Traditional Southern fare was definitely not my favorite, and South side was known to specialize in soul food.

Our horses walked behind us into the backyard of a small white house. My confusion was building. "Tie your horse over here to the fence," my partner directed.

"We can't put our horses by this garden, can we?"

"It'll be fine. Thelma won't mind. Come on."

My uncertainty grew. We had just entered some citizen's private property, tied our horses where they could damage plants and flowers, and walked in the back door. *Why was I always assigned to officers who would not do the right thing?* But instead of the situation being one more in a stack of wrongs, that particular day was a turning point. I would soon receive many life lessons and many blessings that Ms. Thelma would share from our very first meeting.

Through the back door, my partner entered straight into the kitchen where Ms. Thelma welcomed me. I knew immediately I was in the presence of no ordinary person. She nonchalantly accepted the arrival of two police officers through her back door, even when one was white.

"Momma." My partner kissed her on the cheek.

"Who have you brought with you, Hugh?"

"This is my new partner."

"Welcome. There is some butter beans and rice on the stove and chicken in the oven. Help her find a plate."

Lesson one began. Entering this home of a black Southern family in a city where shots heard were not from hunting rifles, and a definitive black/white racial line dictated social life, I was immediately welcomed. Hugh promptly placed a plate in my hand and directed me to fill it from an array of pots and pans on the stove. I sat at an intimate small table squeezed in the space between the refrigerator, stove, and sink.

"Get her something to drink," the matriarch ordered.

"Ten-minute rule, Momma." Her son turned to me. "Pop always said that for the first ten minutes in our home, you are a guest. We will serve you. After that, you are family. There are the glasses in the cupboard. Here's the pitcher of sweet tea. Help yourself."

Hugh's father, known as Pop, was one of the first black police officers in a segregated city. Just as I experienced the welcome feast at the kitchen table that day, so had countless others through the years, starting with Pop's contacts on the streets and on the police force. Pastors, church members, and neighbors all knew the special magic of Ms. Thelma's cooking and baking.

The legacy continued as the couple's eight children brought home friends, college roommates, Army buddies, or anybody they felt needed a meal at the family table. Pop's "ten-minute rule" incorporated all visitors into their ever-expanding network. Those of us who withstood the good-natured kidding and banter that were part of the family's normal expression of love became regulars in Ms. Thelma's kitchen.

Outside of my job at the police department, I tended to isolate myself. I struggled with understanding spoken Southern dialect. I tried to discern between good Southern manners and sexual harassment by my male colleagues. This left me exhausted and withdrawn.

So in the weeks after the first visit, I looked forward to the occasional stops at a friendly place. The horses nibbled off some of those lovely plants in the garden, but Ms. Thelma welcomed them and me with her beloved son. With her invitations, I even participated in family meals, contributing salads of my own on holidays.

Lesson two, came during another of our stops. Okra, not butter beans, was among the offerings on the kitchen stove. Okra was not grown in North Dakota. I made two trips to the stove that day. I loved it.

"You're a little hungry today." My partner commented on my obviously increased appetite after we left Ms. Thelma's house that day.

"Was that dark green pod in the pot what is called okra?" I asked.

"Yes."

"I really like it."

"Well, sir. I'll let Thelma know."

The following week Hugh relayed a message to me. "Ms. Thelma called and asked if you would come to dinner today. She said your name is in the pot."

"My name is in the pot? What does that mean?"

"You'll see."

When we arrived, Miss Thelma sent me to the pot on the kitchen stove immediately after entering the house. There sat a whole pot of okra. In that single act, Ms. Thelma shared her intentional love with me in a very special way, and okra would be waiting for me on many more days to come.

I wasn't the sole recipient of her special ways in love. At her eightieth birthday celebration, many people shared their stories of her subtle actions that poured volumes of love into our hearts. Her hands embraced our hands when we relaxed next to her on the couch. Her biscuits had the fire department repeatedly packed in her tiny kitchen. Her pots and pans were the tools by which she served us from her Christian hands.

The third lesson I learned from her indicated the depth of Ms. Thelma's faith.

"My Great Physician takes care of me. He gives me everything I need," she said.

Ms. Thelma gradually lost most of her sight due to a combination of cataracts and glaucoma. A detriment to a woman who spent hours in her kitchen, the loss of sight, despite three surgeries, forced her to relinquish cooking to her grown children. She couldn't see the difference between salt and sugar, and the risk of burns and other kitchen accidents sidelined Ms. Thelma to the couch.

But even this she handled with grace. She viewed her Lord as her true healer. She took the change in stride by asking her sons and daughters to love her the same as she had loved others all those years, by cooking.

When Ms. Thelma welcomed my mother on her first visit from North Dakota, she stated, "You sit here with me." Ms. Thelma indicated a place beside her on the couch. I was promptly sent back to the kitchen with the rest of her children.

"I know she has a family back in North Dakota," Ms. Thelma shared, "but I think of her as my ninth child. So you don't have to worry about her. She has a family right here in South Carolina."

My own mother was overwhelmed. "Thank you. I can see how well my daughter is loved here. I know she is in good hands."

I loved Ms. Thelma's relationship with Jesus Christ, and I loved God more for giving her to me as my second mother.

In time, she asked me, "When am I going to put my name on you?"

Her question had me speechless as the fourth lesson became clear. Without our ever discussing the change of my relationship with her son from work partner to best friend and life partner, Ms. Thelma determined that she wanted me to share the family name. She chose to cleave herself unto this name by eloping at a very young age. Just as Naomi and Ruth forged a bond so strong despite the disparity of age and culture in Biblical times, Ms. Thelma indicated to me that age, race, and former marriages were not barriers to her son and me marrying. She accepted and knew our hearts and the strength of love which had grown between us. She judged not.

One day amidst the decline of her health and before another heart procedure shortly before her death, Ms. Thelma revealed my fifth lesson in her typical storytelling fashion.

At the same small kitchen table where we ate, she began. "I always had my husband's meal ready for him when he came home from work. One night, I made fried chicken, lima beans with rice, biscuits, and a cold glass of iced tea and sat it before him. The condensation rolled down the side of the glass, but instead of taking a drink or a bite, he took one look at the meal and pushed it away. He got up and walked back out the door without a word. I told the kids to leave that plate and tea alone. Just set them on top of the refrigerator.

"The next night Pop came home and sat down to the table. The meal and tea were taken from atop the refrigerator and served to him. He didn't say a word, just got up and walked away. The meal went back on top of the refrigerator.

"That night shift must have been mighty long for him without dinner in his belly. He was a big, strong man who loved his home-cooked meals. I knew things could be hard out there on him, but we could only survive as a family if we talked to each other.

"On the third night, the same meal was placed on the table before him. A film had formed on the sweet tea, white fur covered the lima beans, the biscuit was dried and hardened, and the chicken smelled odd."

Finally, Pop asked, "Thelma, will I ever get something different to eat?"

"Yes, sir. Just as soon as you open your mouth to speak. You must leave that police business outside this house. When you enter the door, don't drag it home to the kitchen table. No matter what happens, you need to talk here to me."

The audience of four at her table laughed at the image of this kind woman's diligence in teaching her big, brave husband a lesson. I appreciated the glimpse into the respect my husband's parents held for each other.

Hugh had often shared memories of the two holding hands. His mother would sit on his father's lap as she caressed his head. Hugh smiled as he said, "We would call them Romeo and Juliet."

When Ms. Thelma died, we held a celebration of her life. Beautiful flowers adorned the church as one of her sons, a talented African Methodist Episcopalian pastor delivered a wonderful eulogy depicting Ms. Thelma in heaven getting her just dessert. The fork, already placed in her casket,) was in preparation for it.

Without a doubt, the Great Physician welcomed her to her heavenly home. Her precious son, named after her daddy, sat next to me as my husband. And for me, I had no questions as to the cause of her death—Ms. Thelma simply wore out her heart by loving us all so well.

Mamaleh's Lament

by Collette Inez

(from journal notes)
January 14, 1986

Saul's *mamaleh* is sped by ambulance to the hospital for emergency surgery. An intestinal obstruction. The doctors find adhesions from old scars, souvenirs of a hernia correction two years earlier. Surgery has led to more surgery. Saul and I are sobered by the news that an irregular heartbeat keeps her in the Intensive Care Unit. Poor Sylvia, what an insult to her body.

Only the other night she complained of an upset stomach after eating a hot dog. But we had dismissed it as more petulance.

The doctor reassures us she came through surgery nicely, and the prognosis is good for a complete recovery. Mamaleh, eighty-four years old. The nurses are feeding her heart medication to which she is responding. Saul sees her tonight, we visit her together tomorrow.

I think of my own mother who at Sylvia's age is a recluse moving slowly from room to room on a cane; her legs are beginning to wither. If Sylvia had not survived the surgeon's knife, we would have only Marthe, my cool and reluctant single parent in France, who rarely writes and still will not admit I am her daughter. Saul and I, a childless couple, are sole offsprings of our parents. We came from these mothers from nothingness, lived inside these women whose bodies are now betrayed by age.

January 17

Saul receives no news of mamaleh. Her doctors are gone for the weekend. We dine this evening on tempura at Aki's amid distracting concerns for her recovery. When will she leave the ICU? Will she need a pacemaker? When will the tubes be removed? How much longer will she have to stay in Brooklyn's Kings Highway hospital?

We visit her the next day. Her condition has stabilized. In the ICU, elderly patients rasp, mutter, wheeze, and snore in a world of sighing machines, of beeps and clicks. A green video screen with sinuous lines and blips records mamaleh's heartbeat. Another woman, an ancient Sheba, is in an oxygen tent, the others curled in white sheets like sea cows, manatees.

They suffer the disfigurements of age, but less so mamaleh, who greets us wearily, bare-legged in a cotton shift. A tube threads through a nostril and down her throat, deep into the gut that gets no nourishment but glucose in an intravenous cocktail of calcium and water, survival levels. Even in this extremity, she is a good-looking woman. Nature still favors a face which is mostly unwrinkled, a face with a delicate pink nose, eyes half-shut and hazed.

Less attractive are her unrelieved crankiness and insults. She feels no need to act nobly or well. All courtesies are suppressed. She accuses Saul—who took nothing more than a mint to freshen his mouth—of drunkenness, and me of not knowing his breath is liquor-fouled, because I, too, have imbibed. I see this moment of displaced, paranoid anger as boding ill for mamaleh's future. After a great effort to get to the hospital—traffic jams, parking—we leave full of excuses for her behavior, but are, all the same, frustrated and furious during the long trip home.

January 18

Today she is transferred from the ICU to a semi-private room where she claims misery for want of fresh air and for the tormenting clicks of the other patient's monitoring machine. When we last called, she was placed on a respirator to resist her shortness of breath. Never a reliable reporter, she insists that when begging a nurse to take pity on her, the reply was, "Here, there is no pity."

Her condition is fair, but her wretchedness seems critical as she weeps into the telephone. To ease her distress, we have hired a registered nurse to attend her at night: Mrs. James, Jamaican, intelligent. Her pleasantly inflected speech reassures us. But now, mamaleh insists she can neither understand the Chinese accent of Dr. Chan, her family physician, nor Mrs. James's Island lilt.

January 29

She remains in the hospital. Cystoscopy, allergic reactions, catheters, lazy bladder, tongue blisters, gas, IVs. The surgeon, urologist, and internist make their rounds, medical high priests with their incantations, their mumbled abstractions and evasive words. We whirl with their phrases in our ears.

Daily phone calls, anxieties, her frets, her tears; Dr. Chan's laconic English is hard to unscramble. Mrs. James (who mamaleh claims cheats her by diverting paid time to filing her nails), joins her Jamaican sentences to mamaleh's Yiddish whine, sounding a strange orchestration, a bizarre music in this medical concert hall.

But these days, the alliance between the old and their doctors patches up the aged like mechanics tuning up run-down cars at a local garage. I tell this to Saul, who suspects his mother's end may be near. But he finally concedes she will recover and live crabbily to ninety-eight, twenty years longer than her own mother, Chaya, who died swiftly of pneumonia in a Polish shtetl, shortly before the family was gassed at Auschwitz. Of Chaya's thirteen children, Sylvia, the youngest, is the lone survivor.

January 31

Day seventeen at the hospital. She revives from anesthesia given for a cystoscopy. No tumors ride her bladder whose laziness results from age and inactivity, doctors tell us. She complains about the food, eating it nonetheless. Hospitals, one of which claimed Saul's father five years ago, are unhealthy places I say to myself, and I vow to keep them at a distance.

Perhaps this will be her last week of confinement. We ready ourselves for arranging home care. I fixate too much on the money it's costing, the portion of the bills we may have to pay: fees for a second anesthetist, the urologist, the dermatologist, the allergist, the surgeon, Dr. Chan, the scores of tests, X-rays, cardiograms, intensive care extras, the room itself, medications.

Returning home after a Saturday visit, an exasperated Saul describes his mother as a "querulous, petulant child, totally self-absorbed," an "octogenarian going on five."

February 4

Mamaleh will be discharged from the hospital next Thursday. She will leave with a catheter and a urine bag, but seems prepared for her trip home. Saul has retained a Ms. Williams to spend eight hours a day with mamaleh for a month or longer until her muscles strengthen and she can manage on her own.

Exhausting business. I stay up half the night with concerns about our own old age and infirmity, the sinking knowledge that these women, my mother and mamaleh, will enter the earth without understanding me, that there is no hope for beneficent mothering, for realizing childhood's fantasy of a calm and anchoring mother/daughter love. I will always remain outside of that richness.

February 5

Mamaleh in a white hospital gown is perched on the bed, her legs spread, her feet bare. I avert my eyes from what must be sagging folds of flesh, her private parts now poked into three times daily by nurses inserting catheters to pass her urine.
Her legs are white, smooth-skinned and heavyset for her frail and stooped build. In her overheated, semi-private room, a stroke victim lies open-mouthed and toothless, an air compressor sighing like the plangent breathing of a huge animal.

We meet Ms. Williams, another soft Jamaican woman in her late twenties whose composure befits the calm motions of her body's wide curves, a pretty woman who tells me of her children in school.

Who cares for them when she cares for others?

When Ms. Williams leaves to order a wheelchair to exit the hospital, mamaleh whispers to me, "This black woman is too fat. How will she fit into the apartment?" I advise her to hope she has an equally fat heart and fat patience and not to worry about her dress size.

Dazed and anxious, she retreats into her narrow universe of vexations and fears. Yet her mind comes to life when we help her up the flights to her tiny rooms whose walls are crowded with carefully made portraits and landscapes she painted at the senior citizen center, to her unfinished sewing neatly piled next to the ancient Singer machine, to her doll-like rooms whose tan carpet has been thinned by forty-three years of twice-weekly vacuuming.

Separated from Saul's late father for fifty years, she takes pride in living alone as a measure of independence. Alert, she recognizes the territory of her nest without admitting her relief at being home.

I am angry at her ceaseless crotchets and protests, yet feel compassion for her suffering, her recalcitrant bladder, the indignities she has endured.

Dorothy Williams appears accepting and accustomed to these immigrant and sometimes tyrannical old women who cleave to life and take comfort in their world's constricted pleasures.

Hours later, the visiting public nurse, Ms. Baily, a no-nonsense woman, bursts into the apartment in a lively gust of fury. She had been given the wrong address, the wrong phone number, and was "freezing my ass off on the street."

Nurse Baily will teach Dorothy the art of inserting a catheter in her patient three times a day. Mamaleh will get her mothering from a West Indian ladle, a Trinidadian and Jamaican stockpot.

March 10

Our phone talks narrow to her dirty scatter rugs—she is too weak for their frequent washing in the bathtub—to flatulence, bloating after dinners of pureed foods, blood in the stools (she's prone to hemorrhoids), poor sleep, insufficient steam heat, sawdust in the lobby the landlord won't sweep, and so on. But she is healing, taking the stairs and broiling meat patties from which every speck of fat and gristle is laboriously plucked with a pair of tweezers.

We couldn't know that four years of abdominal blockages would follow. Even as she weakened after each surgical procedure, in her railing at doctors and hired nurses with convulsive tears, in her wrath and ferocity, she sustained our faith in her tenacity to survive by rallying after every assault on her body.

April 25, 1990

Saul returns her home after yet another hospital stay. She behaves no differently than before, disconcerted and confused, vigilant only when sending off her nurse companion to an Avenue J grocery with a shopping list of foods. Saul leaves for Manhattan as she inspects, with dismay, the fast approaching expiration date on a container of cottage cheese just purchased.

All is normal. We will call tomorrow.

April 26

We wake on an unseasonably hot morning to a message left on our telephone answering machine. Mamaleh sounds rational, her voice oddly coherent. She will lift herself to the window ledge and leap three stories down to her death.

"Come my children, come to me in the back yard. I am tired. Forgive me, I am going now. Have a good life."

After *Mameleh* Flew Four Floors Down out the Window
(for my mother-in-law) by Colette Inez

We sold her furniture to the landlord.
The dust she despised gathered in the broom of a Pakistani
mother.
The lumpy brown couch welcomed this woman and
her husband.
They stared at the TV Mameleh claimed sent dangerous rays.
In a bed soft with years of restless sleep, this pair turned to one
another.
The children they made banged drawers of the cherry wood
dresser where
photographs from the Polish Pale faded to sepia.
Posed, the sisters linked arms in a blazing summer field,
One escaping to America, the others seized for
Auschwitz freight.
One day leaning out the window, fingertips dusted with curry,
the children call:
"Ami, come look, an old woman is flying over Avenue J."
"She floats in your dream of a cold country," the mother tells
them in Urdu,
buttoning a sweater over her tunic.
They all take bites of warm *chapatis*, stir sugar for the
tamarind tea.

Dear Mother-in-Law

by Sandy Richardson

I spoke with the *real* you—the person God intended you to be—only once. Imagine that—only once in the thirty-five years I knew you before your death. I'll never forget it.

I was alone in a hospital room during the early morning hours. My newborn son was eight hours old, beautiful and perfect. At that time of morning, most of the world sleeps. But not you. You rarely slept. I often wondered why. Was it fear that somewhere in your dreams you would meet the demon that possessed your days? I will never know for sure because you are gone, and you will never confront the reality of who and what you really were, at least not on this earth.

But I called you that night from the hospital. At the time, I still thought I could reach you, could break down your walls. I called because I needed and wanted to talk to someone, and you were the only person I could be sure was awake. I hoped that with the birth of this last child, perhaps things might change.

And for just that one night, I believe the *real* you spoke to me. I still cling to that. You listened patiently, allowing me time to voice my hopes, my fears. I wondered then, as I still do, what triggered those few genuine moments between us. None of your children or grandchildren can remember ever having met *that* you.

"You will love this child beyond your wildest imaginings," you said to me.

You were right. I did and still do. I wish you had learned to do the same for your own child, my husband. Perhaps at his birth, in your heart of hearts, your cruel self stepped to the side for just a moment and allowed the real you to peer down at him.

But it certainly didn't last long because the cruel you soon took charge to verbally and emotionally abuse your son, even in his earliest memories.

"You'd better behave, or I'll send you away. People will say you are crazy," you warned him.

The cruel you stole so much from all of us. What she robbed you of is beyond calculation.

Still, there must have been a moment, one single, golden moment, when you gazed into your son's face and felt the sheer power and beauty of a mother's love. If this had not been so, you could not have responded so understandingly to me that night when my own "mother's heart" reached out to you.

Over the years as your personality grew more destructive, I held fast to the memory of that meeting. That single memory always kept me trying to reach you again, to glimpse the *real* you one more time. I suppose I felt if I just tried hard enough and long enough, the real you might come back. I think we all hoped that, prayed for that. But then again, it is quite possible that in our patience with you, in our love for you, in our excusing, placating, shielding of you, we are, in part, to blame. Perhaps we should not have protected you from yourself and what you were doing to us.

But we did.

And for years, that single memory of the real you saved me from turning my back on the hateful person you were.

Others will shudder at that word hateful. That's because they do not know. They did not live with your meanness. You were so clever in your dealings with those outside the family. You kept your interactions superficial, short-termed. The cruel you could hide for brief intervals. She was clever.

You always did pride yourself on your cleverness.

Your son says that his earliest memories are of that terrible cleverness. He was never able to please you. You, who were so good with words, twisted each and every one of his into something vile. You turned them around, used them against him, against everyone. You played with double meanings, innuendoes. Your little boy, had no way of fighting that. And neither did we.

Oh, and you even fooled the doctors for a time, but eventually they found you out.

"Even very few professionals know how to deal with your mother-in-law," one said to me. "This person is not crazy. She's mean, narcissistic. She's too sane to commit, yet too disturbed to maintain healthy, productive relationships. She cares only for herself, her needs, and her desires. We can't fix that."

And you didn't want to be fixed, saw nothing wrong with yourself. You told me once that you never apologized for anything because you never did anything to apologize for. How were we to find a way around that?

While there was no fix for you, medications could have helped some, but only if you had been willing. You weren't. And no one insisted. Those of us closest to you struggled to do the right thing, the proper thing, the "socially-acceptable" thing, and continued to live with you, tried to defend you, tried to love you.

And I, well, I clung to that one memory of the real you.

I remember again your words that night. "You will love this child beyond your wildest imaginings."

I wish you could go back to the growing years of your own son and love him that way. I wish you could erase the insults, the ridicule, the deceit, the neglect, all the abuses you heaped on his little boy's heart.

I wish you could take back all the "you can'ts" you threw at him.

I wish you could replace all the trust you stole from him.

I wish you could give him back his joy, confidence, and openness. I wish, even now, you could appreciate what a fine man he is in spite of all you did.

I so wish you could have truly loved him, like a mother should love her child.

For you were his mother and ever will be his mother. And HE loved YOU. Yes, in spite of it all, he loved you and still does.

When you and I first met (not the *real* you, the other one) there were no words. You ignored me, wouldn't speak to me, would not even look at me for the whole hour we sat in your living room. You were deliberately rude and cruel to me while you berated your son about how he was wasting his life. I didn't understand why you said those things, but you knew exactly what you were doing.

And your words to me and about me came soon enough.

"Do you understand how difficult it will be for my son to adjust to marriage to you? You are a stranger to us."

"Are you saying you don't approve of our marriage?" I asked.

"I didn't say *that*," you replied and ended the conversation.

When our daughter was born on your birthday, instead of joy and congratulations, you greeted her with, "No one likes to share a birthday."

"Isn't she beautiful?" your son asked.

"Beauty's in the eye of the beholder," you answered. And ever after, you made her birthday difficult for all of us because it was yours, and you could.

One summer early on in my marriage, a friend's child died, and I cut our family vacation short by one day to attend the funeral. In your anger at my leaving, you said I needed to get my priorities in order. It was the last family vacation we ever took with you.

"This work is beneath you," you said to your son about his landscaping business. Then turning to me, you smiled and said, "You've certainly had a strong influence on him."

You told so many lies to all of us, lies meant to drive wedges between each member of your own family. But at least you were fair in this. You didn't lie to just one; you lied to all of us.

Then one day, I still don't know why, you went to visit my grandmother. You had met her only twice. She was ninety-two at the time and blind. You took her a bowl of soup and left assuring her that, in spite of the fact that I was married to your son, you didn't intend to "keep up" my whole family. She was confused by what you said and tried to convince herself that, surely, she must have misunderstood you. But she knew she hadn't, and I knew it, too.

Why did you do that? She never asked anything of you, didn't need anything from you, didn't want anything from you. None of my family did. But you wanted to pretend they did. You wanted to make them match your lies.

What gifts you gave my husband and I were always less than second thoughts. A truly warm smile would have been enough. One *pleasant, normal* holiday or birthday would have been wonderful. But there were none.

Isn't that sad? Out of almost forty years of memories, none of us can remember one single, pleasant special day with you.

But we all continued to try to make something of the devastation you wrought. We tried so hard to find meaningful gifts for you on holidays and special remembrances at other times. But even a simple 'thanks' never came from you.

And because we taught them to enjoy *giving*, our children took joy in offering you presents. But they invariably left in disappointment. You refused to even open the gifts in front of them. Did you understand at all how much that hurt them? What that stole from them?

When your husband, the man who loved and protected you all those years, the father of your children, became ill, he called *me* to come help him off the floor when he fell. You had refused him. And while I struggled to lift him from the floor, you yelled at him from the doorway, humiliating him, mocking his condition and his seventeen years of service to our state, "Get up by yourself, or I'll put a diaper on you and stick you in a wheelchair and walk you down the street so all the neighbors can see, Mr. Senator."

He and I both cried in front of you that day, but you—you just turned and walked away.

Afterward, when it became obvious that he would not recover, you could easily have afforded to have him cared for at home. But no, you sent him to a nursing home in another city, some distance from us, his family, and his friends. You sent him away to be alone.

"I see no reason to rearrange *my* life just because *he* is sick. He'll be embarrassed to have people see him this way," was your reasoning. My husband traveled the hundred miles each and every day to visit his father.

Pops died a few months later with his sons by his side. You had gone home earlier because, as you told us, "There's nothing I can do here."

After his death, I thought the real you might surface, that you might truly want and need us in your life. In his goodness, your husband had been your main protector. I thought, hoped, and prayed, that when left alone, you would see that you needed to change. I hoped we could still salvage something, still somehow make a family with you.

I stood by your side for almost two weeks—stayed in your home, cooked your meals, ran errands, greeted visitors. I held your hand through the funeral service. Not once did you cry. Not once did you reach out to your children or grandchildren to comfort them. Not once did you let them comfort you. But you did mention, time and again, how inconvenient it all was, how hot it was, how tired you were.

It was always all about you.

Then came your accusations that your sons were stealing your inheritance, your lies to neighbors and family friends, your insulting remarks about your deceased husband. You drove everyone away. Your tantrums, lies, schemes, meanness, and madness finally won. Even your grandchildren, grown by then, could no longer cope with your viciousness. We all stopped visiting you. We could not bear the weight of all of that darkness. We had tried. We had failed.

Except for your hired sitters, you stayed alone. They waited on you day and night. You stayed in your bedroom, smoking your cigarettes, scheming, cursing, falsely accusing all, even the walls around you. Your sitters called us in tears, but we had to admit to them we had no influence with you, could not legally do one thing to help. You had appointed a niece who lived in another town as your legal representative.

I can't help but wonder if there were ever any nights, when you in your sleeplessness, may have recognized deep inside how lonely you must have been. Surely there were times when you wanted and needed to talk honestly with someone.

I sometimes imagined the phone would ring, and I would answer, and on the other end of the line would be the woman I met that one night so many years ago.

"It's me," you'd whisper. "I can't sleep. Can we talk?"

But those were only my imaginings, futile wishes, lost dreams. The few times you did call, it wasn't the real you. Your words were not soft or gentle. They remained cruel, vicious, hate-filled, and self-serving.

We heard no words of pride when your son won awards for his business. Nor were there any words of sympathy when my father and my grandmother died. Your grandchildren received no well wishes or congratulations when they left for college. You never even acknowledged the successes in their lives.

And so, the nights and days continued to slip away. The niece you appointed as Power of Attorney allowed you to stay at home on your own. Some of the sitters stole from you. You fell. You dropped a cigarette and burned your carpet and almost caught the house on fire. You left the bath water running and flooded the downstairs. The police responded twice to your home after calls from your caretakers. They had to force you to pay the sitters what you owed them.

I worried about you, and so I called that niece of yours, the one you thought so highly of. I told her we, your children, were concerned. She said she'd look into it.

But I think she surprised even you by doing what you never wanted. She sold your home. She hired strangers to go through your drawers, cabinets, and closets. They tossed your personal mementos away.

Worse, they threw away priceless memories of your son's father—stuffed his things into garbage bags and put them on the street as trash. My husband and I happened to ride by your house the next day. We saw the garbage bags, the empty house, and stopped. And while he sifted and sorted through his father's memories, I held your son while he cried.

Your niece didn't consult with us about her decisions. She merely informed us over the phone after they were made. And then she decreed that you could not leave the nursing home with anyone but her, not even your sons, assuming they wanted to take you out. She hung photos of herself and her family in your room, but none of your own children or grandchildren. She continued the games you began.

She did keep your sitters for you. You always did so hate to be alone. They kept records of who visited and when. But few of the sitters stayed very long. There was a constant flow of new faces, for they, too, grew weary of your meanness.

The day before you died, my daughter and my husband visited you at the hospital. They had to insist that the sitter leave so they could have a few moments alone with you. They shared words, emotions, tears, and prayers you probably weren't conscious of, but I can certainly hope you heard the words they said. I hope that the sense of hearing was left for you to know those few moments of honesty and love, hurt and forgiveness.

Now that you are gone, I will never know if you ever realized all that you missed or how much we all missed because of you?

Your son tries hard not to think about the past. He says he doesn't want to remember. He prays that he has put the worst of the hurts behind him. But hurts do, at times, resurface. They come back in dreams, in moments of abject sorrow and yearning. I see it clearly in his eyes.

I sometimes feel sorry for you. I sometimes blame us. Perhaps we should have forced you to get help. But how? We console ourselves now with the knowledge that, ultimately, some of these things were a result of your own choices. You refused help.

So, we try to hold on to the belief you were ill. We don't want to remember you as hateful and heartless. We don't want to think of you as evil.

But sometimes, we do.

I believe that we have a choice in how we live our lives: either by reaching out and loving others or by shutting ourselves away in bitterness and anger.

I so wished you could have chosen better.

And then more than a year after your death, we sorted through some old books in a box taken from the storage unit your niece finally turned over to us. Tucked inside the pages were loose bits of note paper. I recognized your writing in the lists of "Beauty Tricks for Older Women," and notes on "How to Stay Fashionable in Your Golden Years."

I found copied prayers mixed in with those. I don't remember ever seeing you pray, but there they were—prayers for health, security, and blessings written stingily across the lines. Prayers filled with "me, me, me."

But none for your friends, your caretakers, your family. Not one.

When I set the empty box aside to throw away, something caught my eye—it was one last note, crimped and wedged under the bottom folds of the box. I pulled it out and smoothed the wrinkles. And there in faded blue ink, I think I might have glimpsed the real you one more time. She hid behind four little words:

"I am so afraid."

They reminded me of something suggested by one of your doctors or a friend. Or perhaps it was just a random passage I read. Nevertheless, my mind latched on to it. I don't recall the exact words, but it went something like this:

All people, no matter how negatively they treat others, have two great desires: the desire to be known and the desire to be loved in spite of it.

But I have come to believe that some poor souls never recognize when they are.

I still pray for you.

About the Contributors

Bobbi Adams is a magna cum laude graduate of Wheaton College in zoology. She earned a graduate degree in studio art at NYU. Adams is a Clemson trained Master Gardener and Master Naturalist. Her column, "The Peripatetic Gardener," appears weekly (since 1998) in the Lee County Observer. Her first book, *Gatherings from the Garden*, was published in 2013, and a second book, *Gatherings from the Garden, Volume 2* will include her piece published here. Visit her at www.bobbiadams.com.

Clemson University graduate **Dale Barwick** lives in South Carolina where she works as a Nurse Practitioner. She is a member of the South Carolina Writers Workshop. When she isn't taking care of sick people, she enjoys writing essays and short stories and is currently working on a novel. She lives with her husband, two college-age children, and two spoiled black labs.

Lillian McCarter Batarseh's poem "Apostrophe to Catherine" won third place in the 2010 Sidney Lanier Award Poetry Competition, and her memoir *True Grits* was published online in January 2011 by *Southern Women's Review*. She participated in *The Swamp Fox Writing Project* and *The Advanced Institute* at Francis Marion University and continues to practice her craft as a member and current facilitator of FloWriters, a South Carolina writers' group.

Margaret Jean Bell retired recently after forty years of work in multiple prisons, several psych hospitals, and one heroin clinic. Now in her leisure years, she continues to follow human complexity through her rigorous viewing schedule of reality television.

She notes here her appreciation for her husband's moderate comfort level in the sharing of her essay, "Family Time," and the imperfections of their family. However, she hopes that their children will actually value the complexity of their family's history, flaws and all.

Margaret Jean's interest in personal dynamics is the focus of her first novel, *PRISON GRITS* which was published in 2015. She is presently at work on her second.

Krista Bowes first met her mother-in-law when she began dating her son in ninth grade. Eight years and a few rocky bumps later, they made it official. After twelve years of moving in the Air Force, Krista and her mother-in-law are thrilled to be only two and half hours apart and see each other about every three weeks— or whenever Gigi needs a granddaughter fix. Krista and her family live in South Carolina with a much loved twelve-year-old lab named Bailey.

Kathy China lives in South Carolina with her loving husband, a Siamese cat, and two horses. No longer in law enforcement, she is self-employed as a licensed massage therapist, certified fitness trainer, and registered yoga teacher, 500 – hour level. Her publishing credits include the *Southern Sampler* anthologies and *Wee*

Wisdom in the fifth grade. To see her poem in print at a young age was a significant factor in her writing interest.

Noa Daniels' first book of contemporary poetry *The Common Ground* was published in Spring 2014. She is currently working on her second of three books, *Tear drops and Heart beats.* Noa's poetry is a journey through girlhood to adulthood, painting pictures with words and capturing the emotions of moments in time. Her poems, *Edisto,* and *Caution,* have been featured in Wake Magazine. She frequently blogs on Good Reads and is a supporter of the Writers, Agents, and Editor's Network.
She may be contacted at noadanielsemail@gmail.com.

Lois Rauch Gibson is Professor Emerita of English at Coker College in Hartsville, SC. Since 2012, she spends part of each year in Dar es Salaam, Tanzania, in East Africa. She continues to write, edit, tutor, and serve on community and professional boards on both continents, and to be involved in the international Children's Literature Association.

Before **KIRSTEN GUENTHER** turned playwright, she lived in Paris where she worked as a Paris Correspondent for *BonjourParis.com* and wrote the City Guide for *USA TODAY.com.* While in Paris, she penned the popular weekly column, "The Sexy Expat," about an American journalist trying to navigate the French. Current theatre commissions include the book for MGM's upcoming *Benny & Joon* and the new musical *Measure of Success* (Rockefeller Fellowship). She wrote the book and lyrics for *Little Miss Fix-it* (as seen on *NBC*); and book for *Mrs. Sharp*

(Richard Rodgers Award, starred Jane Krakowski); *Out of My Head* (licensed by Steelespring Stage Rights); and *The Cable Car Nymphomaniac* (Bay Area Theatre Award Nom). She wrote the lyrics for the hit cabaret song, "Accident Prone" with music by Laurence O'Keefe, which has sold thousands of copies and is published by Samuel French. Additionally, she has written sketches and songs for celebrities such as James Franco, Jared Leto, Christopher Walken, Michael Douglas, Catherine Zeta-Jones, Kathie Lee & Hoda, Steve Buscemi, Deion Sanders, Arianna Huffington, Cyndi Lauper, and Queen Latifah, among others. Kirsten was a Dramatist Guild Fellow, and her work has been heard in venues throughout New York City including Joe's Pub, 54 Below, The Public, and Lincoln Center. She holds a BFA from USC and an MFA in Musical Theatre Writing from NYU.

Roxie Ann Hunter is a writer, career counselor, and doting cat mother. She lives in a beautiful brownstone in Brooklyn and is proud to have survived life with a mother-in-law.

Author **Colette Inez** has authored ten poetry collections, most recently *Horseplay* from Word Press. She is widely anthologized and received fellowships from the Guggenheim and Rockefeller Foundations, twice from the NEA, and won two Pushcart prizes. Formerly a visiting professor at Cornell, Ohio, Bucknell, and Colgate Universities, she long taught at Columbia University and appeared on public radio and TV. The University of Wisconsin Press published her memoir *The Secret of M. Dulong*, and her poetry has been set to music by Pulitzer Prize Composer David Del Tredici in *Miz Inez Sez*, a song cycle performed in New York's

Symphony Space, Miller Theater, and elsewhere. An eleventh collection *The Luba Poems* from Red Hen Press was released in early 2015. The poem "After *Mameleh* Flew Four Floors Down out the Window" was previously published in The Antioch Review, Summer 1991, Vol.49, Number 3.

U.S. speaker, cultural trainer, and lifestyle editor **Barbara Pasquet James** writes about food, fashion, travel, and culture from Paris. As one of the editors who launched, wrote, and updated *USA Today's City Guide To Paris*, her writing and comments have appeared in publications as diverse as *The Robb Report*, *The Georgetowner*, luxury lifestyle magazine *Boulevard France*, prize-winning *The American LLC*, and *National Review Online*.

Dianne Johnson (Dinah Johnson) is the author of several picture books including *All Around Town: The Photographs of Richard Samuel Roberts*, *Black Magic* (illustrated by Gregory Christie) and *Quinnie Blue* (illustrated by James Ransome), all published by Henry Holt Books for Young Readers. As an essayist, she contributed to *State of the Heart: South Carolina Writers on the Places They Love* and to *Literary Dogs and Their South Carolina Writers*.

The child of an Army colonel and a teacher, Dianne grew up all around the world, but will always call South Carolina home. So it means a lot to her to have another life as a professor of English at the University of South Carolina. She is a pioneering scholar who was instrumental in uncovering the history of African American children's literature. Dianne's greatest joy is visiting schools and getting letters from children. One of her favorite comments reads: "You had made my heart sing." Visit her at www.dinahjohnsonbooks.com.

Kathryn Etters Lovatt, earned her MA in creative writing and English from Hollins University. She continued her studies at Hong Kong University where she taught in the American Studies Department. A former winner of North Carolina's Doris Betts Prize, she won Press 53's short fiction competition. She has won three Carrie McCray Awards from SC Writers' Workshop. A Virginia Center for the Arts fellow, she received South Carolina Art Commission's Individual Artist grant for prose in 2013. Her work has appeared most recently in *Main Street Rag*, *Moonshine Review*, and *NC Literary Review* on-line as well as in *Serving Up Memory*, an anthology which she co-edited. Kathryn resides in Camden, SC. Contact her at kathrynlovatt@hotmail.com.

Susan Doherty Osteen is an honors graduate of journalism from TCU in Fort Worth, Texas. She has worked for a variety of newspapers and non-profit organizations. In 2010, after more than a decade of collaborative research, she published *Tracing a Legacy*, a 950-page tome chronicling her family's ranching empire from County Donegal, Ireland to the American Wild West. Susan lives in South Carolina with her husband and two children. She continues to write for regional publications and is working on a three-part novel.

Sandy Richardson published her first work of middle grade fiction *The Girl Who Ate Chicken Feet* (Dial Books for Young Readers) in 1998 which received an outstanding merit rating from

Bank Street College's *The Best of Children's Books* (1999). *The Girl Who Ate Chicken Feet* was also nominated for the South Carolina Junior Book Award in 2001-2002.

In addition, her fiction and nonfiction have appeared in several anthologies such as *The Pettigrew Review, Porches: An Anthology, Cows: A Rumination,* and *Beacham's Guide to Literature for Young Adults.* Her articles and essays have also been published on several on-line websites. Her nonfiction essay "Nana's Basket" received a nomination for the Pushcart Prize in 2013.

Sandy is presently at work on completing two middle-grade novels and a short story collection. In July 2016, she took the leap and established her own publishing imprint: Southern Sass Publishing Alliances where she hopes to share great stories from many hearts.

She is a member of the national Society of Children's Book Writers and blogs about writing, life, and other wandering thoughts at www.SouthernSassPublishingAlliances.com and www.SandyRichardson.wordpress.com.

Michelle Ross is a folklorist whose area of interest is narrative presented in every conceivable written or spoken word genre. She received her BA in Interdisciplinary Studies through the University of South Carolina and her MA in Folk Studies through Western Kentucky University. As adjunct faculty for the University of South Carolina Sumter, Michelle teaches *Introduction to Cultural Anthropology* and *Introduction to Folklore Studies.* Because she is adamant that everybody has a story worth telling and preserving, Ross and author Sandy Richardson co-founded two writing workshops: "Leaving a Trace" and "Women's Writing Workshop" (WWW).

She is anticipating the 2017 publication of "Mothers of Angels: Narratives of Life, Death, and Beyond" in *South Carolina Welcomes Y'all: Contemporary Folklife Traditions in South Carolina* (University of South Carolina Press).

Michelle is presently working on an historical fiction stage play titled *Black Sea Sands on Carnahan* which tells the epic story of her Pontian Greek grandparents.

Laura P. Valtorta holds a BA in English from St. Lawrence University, a Masters in English from Duke University, and a Juris Doctorate from the University of South Carolina. Several social work courses also compliment her studies. In her solo law practice, she specializes in employment law, family law, utility law, and Social Security Disability cases. She is also qualified as a mediator in civil cases, state and federal courts, and as an NASD arbitrator.

Laura's publishing credits include *Social Security Disability Practice* (Knowles Publishing 2008), a novel, *Family Meal,* (Carolina Wren Press 1993), and *Start Your Own Law Practice* (Entrepreneur Press 2005). In addition, she contributed a section on Brussels to the *Rough Guide to Belgium, Holland, and the Netherlands* (circa 1988). Several of her short stories have been published in small publications such as *Aethlon* and *The Distillery.*

Since 2013, Laura has been involved in moviemaking. She has produced and directed six films, including **White Rock Boxing**, which aired on South Carolina ETV several times, "Queen of the Road" about a female truck driver, and "The Art House."

End Notes

1. Ernie K-Doe: The Official Mother-in-Law Site—The Man, The Myth, The Legend.; K-Do Publishing; http://www.k-doe.com/bio.shtml
2. Russian Humor; http://www.russia-in-us.com/Humor
3. Piset Wattanavitukul, "The Mother-in-Law Strategy," Awakening Dragon; Asia Pacific Management Forum; http://www.apmforum.com/columns/china11.htm
4. Fikree, Fariyal; Khan, Amanullah; Kadir, Muhammad Masood; Sajan, Fatim; Rahbar, Mohammad H. "What Influences Contraceptive Use Among Young Women in Urban Squatter Settlements of Karachi, Pakistan?" http://www.wellesley.edu/Chinese/Mou/SYau/ClassPara.htm
5. "Modern Korea Still Mothers Moms," http://www.fww.org/../famnews/0627a.html
6. Carney, Kate. "Mrs. Rachel Walker: Paul Revere's Mother-in-Law," http://www.gis.net/~mtf/rwalker.htm

Made in the USA
Columbia, SC
22 July 2018